MONTESSORI'S

Own Handbook

Maria Montessori

IAP © 2009

Montessori, Maria.

Montessori's Own Handbook / Maria Montessori – 1st ed.

1. Education

TO MY DEAR FRIEND

DONNA MARIA MARAINI MARCHIONESS GUERRIERI-GONZAGA

WHO DEVOTEDLY AND WITH SACRIFICE HAS GENEROUSLY UPHELD THIS WORK
OF EDUCATION BROUGHT TO BIRTH IN OUR BELOVED COUNTRY BUT OFFERED
TO THE CHILDREN OF HUMANITY

Note by the Author

As a result of the widespread interest that has been taken in my method of child education, certain books have been issued, which may appear to the general reader to be authoritative expositions of the Montessori system. I wish to state definitely that the present work, the English translation of which has been authorized and approved by me, is the only authentic manual of the Montessori method, and that the only other authentic or authorized works of mine in the English language are "The Montessori Method," and "Pedagogical Anthropology."

Maria Montessori

Preface

If a preface is a light which should serve to illumine the contents of a volume, I choose, not words, but human figures to illustrate this little book intended to enter families where children are growing up. I therefore recall here, as an eloquent symbol, Helen Keller and Mrs. Anne Sullivan Macy, who are, by their example, both teachers to myself--and, before the world, living documents of the miracle in education.

In fact, Helen Keller is a marvelous example of the phenomenon common to all human beings: the possibility of the liberation of the imprisoned spirit of man by the education of the senses. Here lies the basis of the method of education of which the book gives a succinct idea.

If one only of the senses sufficed to make of Helen Keller a woman of exceptional culture and a writer, who better than she proves the potency of that method of education which builds on the senses? If Helen Keller attained through exquisite natural gifts to an elevated conception of the world, who better than she proves that in the inmost self of man lies the spirit ready to reveal itself?

Helen, clasp to your heart these little children, since they, above all others, will understand you. They are your younger brothers: when, with bandaged eyes and in silence, they touch with their little hands, profound impressions rise in their consciousness, and they exclaim with a new form of happiness: "I see with my hands." They alone, then, can fully understand the drama of the mysterious privilege your soul has known. When, in darkness and in silence, their spirit left free to expand, their intellectual energy redoubled, they become able to read and write without having learnt, almost as it were by intuition, they, only they, can understand in part the ecstasy which God granted you on the luminous path of learning.

MARIA MONTESSORI.

Contents

Introductory Remarks

Recent years have seen a remarkable improvement in the conditions of child life. In all civilized countries, but especially in England, statistics show a decrease in infant mortality.

Related to this decrease in mortality a corresponding improvement is to be seen in the physical development of children; they are physically finer and more vigorous. It has been the diffusion, the popularization of science, which has brought about such notable advantages. Mothers have learned to welcome the dictates of modern hygiene and to put them into practice in bringing up their children. Many new social institutions have sprung up and have been perfected with the object of assisting children and protecting them during the period of physical growth.

In this way what is practically a new race is coming into being, a race more highly developed, finer and more robust; a race which will be capable of offering resistance to insidious disease.

What has science done to effect this? Science has suggested for us certain very simple rules by which the child has been restored as nearly as possible to conditions of a natural life, and an order and a guiding law have been given to the functions of the body. For example, it is science which suggested maternal feeding, the abolition of swaddling clothes, baths, life in the open air, exercise, simple short clothing, quiet and plenty of sleep. Rules were also laid down for the measurement of food adapting it rationally to the physiological needs of the child's life.

Yet with all this, science made no contribution that was entirely new. Mothers had always nursed their children, children had always been clothed, they had breathed and eaten before.

The point is, that the same physical acts which, performed blindly and without order, led to disease and death, when ordered *rationally* were the means of giving strength and life.

* * * * *

The great progress made may perhaps deceive us into thinking that everything possible has been done for children.

We have only to weigh the matter carefully, however, to reflect: Are our children only those healthy little bodies which to-day are growing and developing so vigorously under our eyes? Is their destiny fulfilled in the production of beautiful human bodies?

In that case there would be little difference between their lot and that of the animals which we raise that we may have good meat or beasts of burden.

Man's destiny is evidently other than this, and the care due to the child covers a field wider than that which is considered by physical hygiene. The mother who has given her child his bath and sent him in his perambulator to the park has not fulfilled the mission of the "mother of humanity." The hen which gathers her chickens together, and the cat which licks her kittens and lavishes on them such tender care, differ in no wise from the human mother in the services they render.

No, the human mother if reduced to such limits devotes herself in vain, feels that a higher aspiration has been stifled within her. She is yet the mother of man.

Children must grow not only in the body but in the spirit, and the mother longs to follow the mysterious spiritual journey of the beloved one who to-morrow will be the intelligent, divine creation, man.

Science evidently has not finished its progress. On the contrary, it has scarcely taken the first step in advance, for it has hitherto stopped at the welfare of the body. It must continue, however, to advance; on the same positive lines along which it has improved the health and saved the physical life of the children, it is bound in the future to benefit and to reinforce their inner life, which is the real *human life*. On the same positive lines science will proceed to direct the development of the intelligence, of character, and of those latent creative forces which lie hidden in the marvelous embryo of man's spirit.

* * * * *

As the child's body must draw nourishment and oxygen from its external environment, in order to accomplish a great physiological work, the *work of growth*, so also the spirit must take from its environment the nourishment which it needs to develop according to its own "laws of growth." It cannot be denied that the phenomena of development are a great work in themselves. The consolidation of the bones, the growth of the whole body, the completion of the minute construction of the brain, the formation of the teeth, all these are very real labors of the physiological organism, as is also the transformation which the organism undergoes during the period of puberty.

These exertions are very different from those put forth by mankind in so-called *external work*, that is to say, in "social production," whether in the schools where man is taught, or in the world where, by the activity of his intelligence, he produces wealth and transforms his environment.

It is none the less true, however, that they are both "work." In fact, the organism during these periods of greatest physiological work is least capable of performing external tasks, and sometimes the work of growth is of such extent and difficulty that the individual is overburdened, as with an excessive strain, and for this reason alone becomes exhausted or even dies.

Man will always be able to avoid "external work" by making use of the labor of others, but there is no possibility of shirking that inner work. Together with birth and death it has been imposed by nature itself, and each man must accomplish it for himself. This difficult, inevitable labor, this is the "work of the child."

When we say then that little children should *rest*, we are referring to one side only of the question of work. We mean that they should rest from that *external* visible work to which the little child through his weakness and incapacity cannot make any contribution useful either to himself or to others.

Our assertion, therefore, is not absolute; the child in reality is not resting, he is performing the mysterious inner work of his autoformation. He is working to make a man, and to accomplish this it is not enough that the child's body should grow in actual size; the most intimate functions of the motor and nervous systems must also be established and the intelligence developed.

The functions to be established by the child fall into two groups: (1) the motor functions by which he is to secure his balance and learn to walk, and to coordinate his movements; (2) the sensory functions through which, receiving sensations from his environment, he lays the foundations of his intelligence by a continual exercise of observation, comparison and judgment. In this way he gradually comes to be acquainted with his environment and to develop his intelligence.

At the same time he is learning a *language,* and he is faced not only with the motor difficulties of articulation, sounds and words, but also with the difficulty of gaining an intelligent understanding of names and of the syntactical composition of the language.

If we think of an emigrant who goes to a new country ignorant of its products, ignorant of its natural appearance and social order, entirely ignorant of its language, we realize that there is an immense work of adaptation which he must perform before he can associate himself with the active life of the unknown people. No one will be able to do for him that work of adaptation. He himself must observe, understand, remember, form judgments, and learn the new language by laborious exercise and long experience.

What is to be said then of the child? What of this emigrant who comes into a new world, who, weak as he is and before his organism is completely developed, *must* in a short time adapt himself to a world so complex?

Up to the present day the little child has not received rational aid in the accomplishment of this laborious task. As regards the psychical development of the child we find ourselves in a period parallel to that in which the physical life was left to the mercy of chance and instinct--the period in which infant mortality was a scourge.

It is by scientific and rational means also that we must facilitate that inner work of psychical adaptation to be accomplished within the child, a work which is by no means the same thing as "any external work or production whatsoever."

This is the aim which underlies my method of infant education, and it is for this reason that certain principles which it enunciates, together with that part which deals with the technique of their practical application, are not of a general character, but have special reference to the particular case of the child from three to seven years of age, *i.e.*, to the needs of a formative period of life.

My method is scientific, both in its substance and in its aim. It makes for the attainment of a more advanced stage of progress, in directions no longer only material and physiological. It is an endeavor to complete the course which hygiene has already taken, but in the treatment of the physical side alone.

If to-day we possessed statistics respecting the nervous debility, defects of speech, errors of perception and of reasoning, and lack of character in normal children, it would perhaps be interesting to compare them with statistics of the same nature, but compiled from the study of children who have had a number of years of rational education. In all probability we should find a striking resemblance between such statistics and those to-day available showing the decrease in mortality and the improvement in the physical development of children.

A Children's House

The "Children's House" is the *environment* which is offered to the child that he may be given the opportunity of developing his activities. This kind of school is not of a fixed type, but may vary according to the financial resources at disposal and to the opportunities afforded by the environment. It ought to be a real house; that is to say, a set of rooms with a garden of which the children are the masters. A garden which contains shelters is ideal, because the children can play or sleep under them, and can also bring their tables out to work or dine. In this way they may live almost entirely in the open air, and are protected at the same time from rain and sun.

The central and principal room of the building, often also the only room at the disposal of the children, is the room for "intellectual work." To this central room can be added other smaller rooms according to the means and opportunities of the place: for example, a bathroom, a dining-room, a little parlor or common-room, a room for manual work, a gymnasium and rest-room.

The special characteristic of the equipment of these houses is that it is adapted for children and not adults. They contain not only didactic material specially fitted for the intellectual development of the child, but also a complete equipment for the management of the miniature family. The furniture is light so that the children can move it about, and it is painted in some light color so that the children can wash it with soap and water. There are low tables of various sizes and shapes--square, rectangular and round, large and small. The rectangular shape is the most common as two or more children can work at it together. The seats are small wooden chairs, but there are also small wicker armchairs and sofas.

FIG. 1.--CUPBOARD WITH APPARATUS.

In the working-room there are two indispensable pieces of furniture. One of these is a very long cupboard with large doors. (Fig. 1.) It is very low so that a small child can set on the top of it small objects such as mats, flowers, etc. Inside this cupboard is kept the didactic material which is the common property of all the children.

The other is a chest of drawers containing two or three columns of little drawers, each of which has a bright handle (or a handle of some color to contrast with the background), and a small card with a name upon it. Every child has his own drawer, in which to put things belonging to him.

Round the walls of the room are fixed blackboards at a low level, so that the children can write or draw on them, and pleasing, artistic pictures, which are changed from time to time as circumstances direct. The pictures represent children, families, landscapes, flowers and fruit, and more often Biblical and historical incidents. Ornamental plants and flowering plants ought always to be placed in the room where the children are at work.

Another part of the working-room's equipment is seen in the pieces of carpet of various colors--red, blue, pink, green and brown. The children spread these rugs upon the floor, sit upon them and work there with the didactic material. A room of this kind is larger than the customary class-rooms, not only because the little tables and separate chairs take up more space, but also because a large part of the floor must be free for the children to spread their rugs and work upon them.

In the sitting-room, or "club-room," a kind of parlor in which the children amuse themselves by conversation, games, or music, etc., the furnishings should be especially tasteful. Little tables of different sizes, little armchairs and sofas should be placed here and there. Many brackets of all kinds and sizes, upon which may be put statuettes, artistic vases or framed photographs, should adorn the walls; and, above all, each child should have a little flower-pot, in which he may sow the seed of some indoor plant, to tend and cultivate it as it grows. On the tables of this sitting-room should be placed large albums of colored pictures, and also games of patience, or various geometric solids, with which the children can play at pleasure, constructing figures, etc. A piano, or, better, other musical instruments, possibly harps of small dimensions, made especially for children, completes the equipment. In this "club-room" the teacher may sometimes entertain the children with stories, which will attract a circle of interested listeners.

The furniture of the dining-room consists, in addition to the tables, of low cupboards accessible to all the children, who can themselves put in their place and take away the crockery, spoons, knives and forks, table-cloth and napkins. The plates are always of china, and the tumblers and water-bottles of glass. Knives are always included in the table equipment.

The Dressing-room. Here each child has his own little cupboard or shelf. In the middle of the room there are very simple washstands, consisting of tables, on each of which stand a small basin, soap and nail-brush. Against the wall stand little sinks with water-taps. Here the children may draw and pour away their water. There is no limit to the equipment of the "Children's Houses" because the children themselves do everything. They sweep the rooms, dust and wash the furniture, polish the brasses, lay and clear away the table, wash up, sweep and roll up the rugs, wash a few little clothes, and cook eggs. As regards their personal toilet, the children know how to dress and undress themselves. They hang their clothes on little hooks, placed very low so as to be within reach of a little child, or else they fold up such articles of clothing, as their little serving-aprons, of which they take great care, and lay them inside a cupboard kept for the household linen.

* * * * *

In short, where the manufacture of toys has been brought to such a point of complication and perfection that children have at their disposal entire dolls' houses, complete wardrobes for the dressing and undressing of dolls, kitchens where they can pretend to cook, toy animals as nearly lifelike as possible, this method seeks to give all this to the child in reality--making him an actor in a living scene.

* * * * *

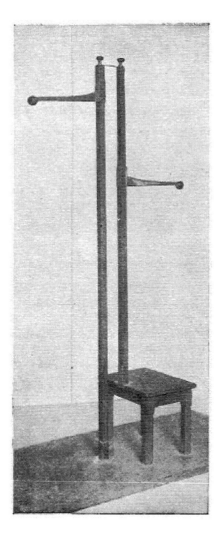

FIG 2.--THE MONTESSORI PAEDOMETER.

My pedometer forms part of the equipment of a "Children's House." After various modifications I have now reduced this instrument to a very practical form. (Fig. 2.)

The purpose of the pedometer, as its name shows, is to measure the children. It consists of a wide rectangular board, forming the base, from the center of which rise two wooden posts held together at the top by a narrow flat piece of metal. To each post is connected a horizontal metal rod--the indicator-- which runs up and down by means of a casing, also of metal. This metal casing is made in one piece with the indicator, to the end of which is fixed an india-rubber ball. On one side, that is to say, behind one of the two tall vertical wooden posts, there is a small seat, also of wood. The two tall wooden posts are graduated. The post to which the seat is fixed is graduated from the surface of the seat to the top, whilst the other is graduated from the wooden board at the base to the top, i.e. to a height of 1.5 meters. On the side containing the seat the height of the child seated is measured, on the other side the child's full stature. The practical value of this instrument lies in the possibility of measuring two children at the

[16]

same time, and in the fact that the children themselves cooperate in taking the measurements. In fact, they learn to take off their shoes and to place themselves in the correct position on the pedometer. They find no difficulty in raising and lowering the metal indicators, which are held so firmly in place by means of the metal casing that they cannot deviate from their horizontal position even when used by inexpert hands. Moreover they run extremely easily, so that very little strength is required to move them. The little india-rubber balls prevent the children from hurting themselves should they inadvertently knock their heads against the metal indicator.

The children are very fond of the pedometer. "Shall we measure ourselves?" is one of the proposals which they make most willingly and with the greatest likelihood of finding many of their companions to join them. They also take great care of the pedometer, dusting it, and polishing its metal parts. All the surfaces of the pedometer are so smooth and well polished that they invite the care that is taken of them, and by their appearance when finished fully repay the trouble taken.

The pedometer represents the scientific part of the method, because it has reference to the anthropological and psychological study made of the children, each of whom has his own biographical record. This biographical record follows the history of the child's development according to the observations which it is possible to make by the application of my method. This subject is dealt with at length in my other books. A series of cinematograph pictures has been taken of the pedometer at a moment when the children are being measured. They are seen coming of their own accord, even the very smallest, to take their places at the instrument.

The Method

The technique of my method as it follows the guidance of the natural physiological and psychical development of the child, may be divided into three parts:

Motor education. Sensory education. Language.

The care and management of the environment itself afford the principal means of motor education, while sensory education and the education of language are provided for by my didactic material.

The didactic material for the *education of the senses* consists of:

(*a*) Three sets of solid insets. (*b*) Three sets of solids in graduated sizes, comprising: (1) Pink cubes. (2) Brown prisms. (3) Rods: (*a*) colored green; (*b*) colored alternately red and blue. (*c*) Various geometric solids (prism, pyramid, sphere, cylinder, cone, etc.). (*d*) Rectangular tablets with rough and smooth surfaces. (*e*) A collection of various stuffs. (*f*) Small wooden tablets of different weights. (*g*) Two boxes, each containing sixty-four colored tablets. (*h*) A chest of drawers containing plane insets. (*i*) Three series of cards on which are pasted geometrical forms in paper. (*k*) A collection of cylindrical closed boxes (sounds). (*l*) A double series of musical bells, wooden boards on which are painted the lines used in music, small wooden discs for the notes.

Didactic Material for the Preparation for Writing and Arithmetic

(*m*) Two sloping desks and various iron insets. (*n*) Cards on which are pasted sandpaper letters. (*o*) Two alphabets of colored cardboard and of different sizes. (*p*) A series of cards on which are pasted sandpaper figures (1, 2, 3, etc.). (*q*) A series of large cards bearing the same figures in smooth paper for the enumeration of numbers above ten. (*r*) Two boxes with small sticks for counting. (*s*) The volume of drawings belonging specially to the method, and colored pencils. (*t*) The frames for lacing, buttoning, etc., which are used for the education of the movements of the hand.

Motor Education

The education of the movements is very complex, as it must correspond to all the coordinated movements which the child has to establish in his physiological organism. The child, if left without guidance, is disorderly in his movements, and these disorderly movements are the *special characteristic of the little child*. In fact, he "never keeps still," and "touches everything." This is what forms the child's so-called "unruliness" and "naughtiness."

The adult would deal with him by checking these movements, with the monotonous and useless repetition "keep still." As a matter of fact, in these movements the little one is seeking the very exercise which will organize and coordinate the movements useful to man. We must, therefore, desist from the useless attempt to reduce the child to a state of immobility. We should rather give "order" to his movements, leading them to those actions towards which his efforts are actually tending. This is the aim of muscular education at this age. Once a direction is given to them, the child's movements are made towards a definite end, so that he himself grows quiet and contented, and becomes an active worker, a being calm and full of joy. This education of the movements is one of the principal factors in producing that outward appearance of "discipline" to be found in the "Children's Houses." I have already spoken at length on this subject in my other books.

Muscular education has reference to:

The primary movements of everyday life (walking, rising, sitting, handling objects). The care of the person. Management of the household. Gardening. Manual work. Gymnastic exercises. Rhythmic movements.

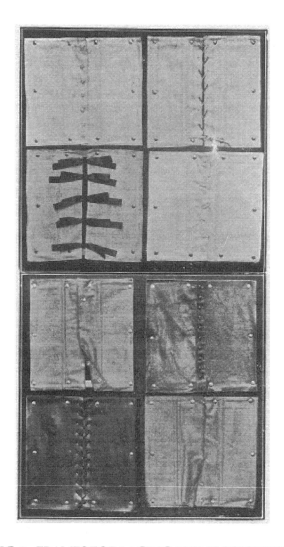

FIG. 3.--FRAMES FOR LACING AND BUTTONING.

In the care of the person the first step is that of dressing and undressing. For this end there is in my didactic material a collection of frames to which are attached pieces of stuff, leather, etc. These can be buttoned, hooked, tied together--in fact, joined in all the different ways which our civilization has invented for fastening our clothing, shoes, etc. (Fig. 3.) The teacher, sitting by the child's side, performs the necessary movements of the fingers very slowly and deliberately, separating the movements themselves into their different parts, and letting them be seen clearly and minutely.

For example, one of the first actions will be the adjustment of the two pieces of stuff in such a way that the edges to be fastened together touch one another from top to bottom. Then, if it is a buttoning-frame, the teacher will show the child the different stages of the action. She will take hold of the button, set it opposite the buttonhole, make it enter the buttonhole completely, and adjust it carefully in its place above. In the same way, to teach a child to tie a bow, she will separate the stage in which he ties the ribbons together from that in which he makes the bows.

[22]

In the cinematograph film there is a picture which shows an entire lesson in the tying of the bows with the ribbons. These lessons are not necessary for all the children, as they learn from one another, and of their own accord come with great patience to analyze the movements, performing them separately very slowly and carefully. The child can sit in a comfortable position and hold his frame on the table. (Fig. 4.) As he fastens and unfastens the same frame many times over with great interest, he acquires an unusual deftness of hand, and becomes possessed with the desire to fasten real clothes whenever he has the opportunity. We see the smallest children *wanting* to dress themselves and their companions. They go in search of amusement of this kind, and defend themselves with all their might against the adult who would try to help them.

FIG. 4.--CHILD BUTTONING ON FRAME. (PHOTO TAKEN AT MR. HAWKER'S SCHOOL AT RUNTON.)

[23]

In the same way for the teaching of the other and larger movements, such as washing, setting the table, etc., the directress must at the beginning intervene, teaching the child with few or no words at all, but with very precise actions. She teaches all the movements: how to sit, to rise from one's seat, to take up and lay down objects, and to offer them gracefully to others. In the same way she teaches the children to set the plates one upon the other and lay them on the table without making any noise.

The children learn easily and show an interest and surprising care in the performance of these actions. In classes where there are many children it is necessary to arrange for the children to take turns in the various household duties, such as housework, serving at table, and washing dishes. The children readily respect such a system of turns. There is no need to ask them to do this work, for they come spontaneously--even little ones of two and a half years old--to offer to do their share, and it is frequently most touching to watch their efforts to imitate, to remember, and, finally, to conquer their difficulty. Professor Jacoby, of New York, was once much moved as he watched a child, who was little more than two years old and not at all intelligent in appearance, standing perplexed, because he could not remember whether the fork should be set at the right hand or the left. He remained a long while meditating and evidently using all the powers of his mind. The other children older than he watched him with admiration, marveling, like ourselves, at the life developing under our eyes.

The instructions of the teacher consist then merely in a hint, a touch--enough to give a start to the child. The rest develops of itself. The children learn from one another and throw themselves into the work with enthusiasm and delight. This atmosphere of quiet activity develops a fellow-feeling, an attitude of mutual aid, and, most wonderful of all, an intelligent interest on the part of the older children in the progress of their little companions. It is enough just to set a child in these peaceful surroundings for him to feel perfectly at home. In the cinematograph pictures the actual work in a "Children's House" may be seen. The children are moving about, each one fulfilling his own task, whilst the teacher is in a corner watching. Pictures were taken also of the children engaged in the care of the house, that is, in the care both of their persons and of their surroundings. They can be seen washing their faces, polishing their shoes, washing the furniture, polishing the metal indicators of the pedometer, brushing the carpets, etc. In the work of laying the table the children are seen quite by themselves, dividing the work among themselves, carrying the plates, spoons, knives and forks, etc., and, finally, sitting down at the tables where the little waitresses serve the hot soup.

Again, gardening and manual work are a great pleasure to our children. Gardening is already well known as a feature of infant education, and it is recognized by all that plants and animals attract the children's care and attention. The ideal of the "Children's Houses" in this respect is to imitate the best in the present usage of those schools which owe their inspiration more or less to Mrs. Latter.

For manual instruction we have chosen clay work, consisting of the construction of little tiles, vases and bricks. These may be made with the help of simple instruments, such as molds. The completion of the work should be the aim always kept in view, and, finally, all the little objects made by the children should be glazed and baked in the furnace. The children themselves learn to line a wall with shining white or colored tiles wrought in various designs, or, with the help of mortar and a trowel, to cover the floor with little bricks. They also dig out foundations and then use their bricks to build division walls, or entire little houses for the chickens.

Among the gymnastic exercises that which must be considered the most important is that of the "line." A line is described in chalk or paint upon a large space of floor. Instead of one line, there may also be two concentric lines, elliptical in form. The children are taught to walk upon these lines like tight-rope walkers, placing their feet one in front of the other. To keep their balance they make efforts exactly similar to those of real tight-rope walkers, except that they have no danger with which to reckon, as the lines are only *drawn* upon the floor. The teacher herself performs the exercise, showing clearly how she sets her feet, and the children imitate her without any necessity for her to speak. At first it is only certain children who follow her, and when she has shown them how to do it, she withdraws, leaving the phenomenon to develop of itself.

The children for the most part continue to walk, adapting their feet with great care to the movement they have seen, and making efforts to keep their balance so as not to fall. Gradually the other children draw near and watch and also make an attempt. Very little time elapses before the whole of the two ellipses or the one line is covered with children balancing themselves, and continuing to walk round, watching their feet with an expression of deep attention on their faces.

Music may then be used. It should be a very simple march, the rhythm of which is not obvious at first, but which accompanies and enlivens the spontaneous efforts of the children.

When they have learned in this way to master their balance the children have brought the act of walking to a remarkable standard of perfection, and have acquired, in addition to security and composure in their natural gait, an unusually graceful carriage of the body. The exercise on the line can afterwards be made more complicated in various ways. The first application is that of calling forth rhythmic exercise by the sound of a march upon the piano. When the same march is repeated during several days, the children end by feeling the rhythm and by following it with movements of their arms and feet. They also accompany the exercises on the line with songs.

Little by little the music is *understood* by the children. They finish, as in Miss George's school at Washington, by singing over their daily work with the didactic material. The "Children's House," then, resembles a hive of bees humming as they work.

As to the little gymnasium, of which I speak in my book on the "Method," one piece of apparatus is particularly practical. This is the "fence," from which the children hang by their arms, freeing their legs from the heavy weight of the body and strengthening the arms. This fence has also the advantage of being useful in a garden for the purpose of dividing one part from another, as, for example, the flower-beds from the garden walks, and it does not detract in any way from the appearance of the garden.

[25]

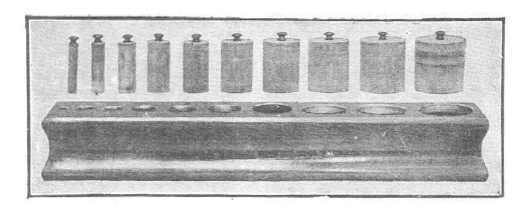

FIG. 5.--CYLINDERS DECREASING IN DIAMETER ONLY.

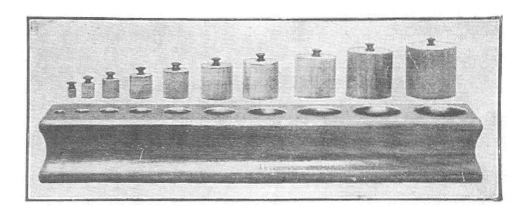

FIG. 6.--CYLINDERS DECREASING IN DIAMETER AND HEIGHT.

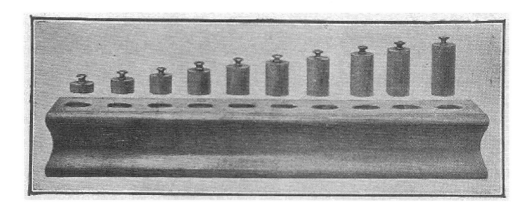

FIG. 7.--CYLINDERS DECREASING IN HEIGHT ONLY.

My didactic material offers to the child the *means* for what may be called "sensory education."

In the box of material the first three objects which are likely to attract the attention of a little child from two and a half to three years old are three solid pieces of wood, in each of which is inserted a row of ten small cylinders, or sometimes discs, all furnished with a button for a handle. In the first case there is a row of cylinders of the same height, but with a diameter which decreases from thick to thin. (Fig. 5.) In the second there are cylinders which decrease in all dimensions, and so are either larger or smaller, but always of the same shape. (Fig. 6.)

Lastly, in the third case, the cylinders have the same diameter but vary in height, so that, as the size decreases, the cylinder gradually becomes a little disc in form. (Fig. 7.)

The first cylinders vary in two dimensions (the section); the second in all three dimensions; the third in one dimension (height). The order which I have given refers to the degree of *ease* with which the child performs the exercises.

The exercise consists in taking out the cylinders, mixing them and putting them back in the right place. It is performed by the child as he sits in a comfortable position at a little table. He exercises his hands in the delicate act of taking hold of the button with the tips of one or two fingers, and in the little movements of the hand and arm as he mixes the cylinders, *without letting them fall* and *without making too much noise* and puts them back again each in its own place.

In these exercises the teacher may, in the first instance, intervene, merely taking out the cylinders, mixing them carefully on the table and then showing the child that he is to put them back, but without performing the action herself. Such intervention, however, is almost always found to be unnecessary, for the children *see* their companions at work, and thus are encouraged to imitate them.

They like to do it *alone*; in fact, sometimes almost in private for fear of inopportune help. (Fig. 8.)

FIG. 8.--CHILD USING CASE OF CYLINDERS.

But how is the child to find the right place for each of the little cylinders which lie mixed upon the table? He first makes trials; it often happens that he places a cylinder which is too large for the empty hole over which he puts it. Then, changing its place, he tries others until the cylinder goes in. Again, the contrary may happen; that is to say, the cylinder may slip too easily into a hole too big for it. In that case it has taken a place which does not belong to it at all, but to a larger cylinder. In this way one cylinder at the end will be left out without a place, and it will not be possible to find one that fits. Here the child cannot help seeing his mistake in concrete form. He is perplexed, his little mind is faced with a problem which interests him intensely. Before, all the cylinders fitted, now there is one that will not fit. The little one stops, frowning, deep in thought. He begins to feel the little buttons and finds that some cylinders have too much room. He thinks that perhaps they are out of their right place and tries to place them correctly. He repeats the process again and again, and finally he succeeds. Then it is that he breaks into a smile of triumph. The exercise arouses the intelligence of the child; he wants to repeat it right from the beginning and, having learned by experience, he makes another attempt. Little children from three to three and a half years old have repeated the exercise up to *forty* times without losing their interest in it.

If the second set of cylinders and then the third are presented, the *change* of shape strikes the child and reawakens his interest.

The material which I have described serves to *educate the eye* to distinguish *difference in dimension*, for the child ends by being able to recognize at a glance the larger or the smaller hole which exactly fits the cylinder which he holds in his hand. The educative process is based on this: that the control of the error lies in *the material itself*, and the child has concrete evidence of it.

The desire of the child to attain an end which he knows, leads him to correct himself. It is not a teacher who makes him notice his mistake and shows him how to correct it, but it is a complex work of the child's own intelligence which leads to such a result.

Hence at this point there begins the process of auto-education.

The aim is not an external one, that is to say, it is *not* the object that the child should learn how to place the cylinders, and *that he should know how to perform an exercise.*

The aim is an inner one, namely, that the child train himself to observe; that he be led to make comparisons between objects, to form judgments, to reason and to decide; and it is in the indefinite repetition of this exercise of attention and of intelligence that a real development ensues.

* * * * *

FIG. 9.--THE TOWER.

The series of objects to follow after the cylinders consists of three sets of geometrical solid forms:

(1) Ten wooden cubes colored pink. The sides of the cubes diminish from ten centimeters to one centimeter. (Fig. 9.)

With these cubes the child builds a tower, first laying on the ground (upon a carpet) the largest cube, and then placing on the top of it all the others in their order of size to the very smallest. (Fig. 10.) As soon as he has built the tower, the child, with a blow of his hand, knocks it down, so that the cubes are scattered on the carpet, and then he builds it up again.

FIG. 10.--CHILD PLAYING WITH TOWER. (PHOTO TAKEN AT MR. HAWKER'S SCHOOL AT RUNTON.)

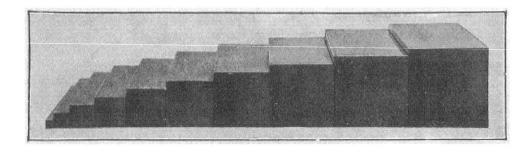

FIG. 11.--THE BROAD STAIR.

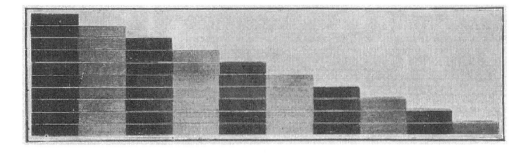

FIG. 12.--THE LONG STAIR.

(2) Ten wooden prisms, colored brown. The length of the prisms is twenty centimeters, and the square section diminishes from ten centimeters a side to the smallest, one centimeter a side. (Fig. 11.)

The child scatters the ten pieces over a light-colored carpet, and then beginning sometimes with the thickest, sometimes with the thinnest, he places them in their right order of gradation upon a table.

(3) Ten rods, colored green, or alternately red and blue, all of which have the same square section of four centimeters a side, but vary by ten centimeters in length from ten centimeters to one meter. (Fig. 12.)

The child scatters the ten rods on a large carpet and mixes them at random, and, by comparing rod with rod, he arranges them according to their order of length, so that they take the form of a set of organ pipes.

As usual, the teacher, by doing the exercises herself, first shows the child how the pieces of each set should be arranged, but it will often happen that the child learns, not directly from her, but by watching his companions. She will, however, always continue to watch the children, never losing sight of their efforts, and any correction of hers will be directed more towards preventing rough or disorderly use of the material than towards any *error* which the child may make in placing the rods in their order of gradation. The reason is that the mistakes which the child makes, by placing, for example, a small cube beneath one that is larger, are caused by his own lack of education, and it is the *repetition of the exercise* which, by refining his powers of observation, will lead him sooner or later to *correct himself*. Sometimes it happens that a child working with the long rods makes the most glaring mistakes. As the aim of the exercise, however, is *not* that the rods be arranged in the right order of gradation, but that the child *should practice by himself*, there is no need to intervene.

One day the child will arrange all the rods in their right order, and then, full of joy, he will call the teacher to come and admire them. The object of the exercise will thus be achieved.

These three sets, the cubes, the prisms, and the rods, cause the child to move about and to handle and carry objects which are difficult for him to grasp with his little hand. Again, by their use, he repeats the *training of the eye* to the recognition of differences of size between similar objects. The exercise would seem easier, from the sensory point of view, than the other with the cylinders described above.

As a matter of fact, it is more difficult, as there is *no control of the error in the material itself*. It is the child's eye alone which can furnish the control.

Hence the difference between the objects should strike the eye at once; for that reason larger objects are used, and the necessary visual power presupposes a previous preparation (provided for in the exercise

[33]

with the solid insets).

* * * * *

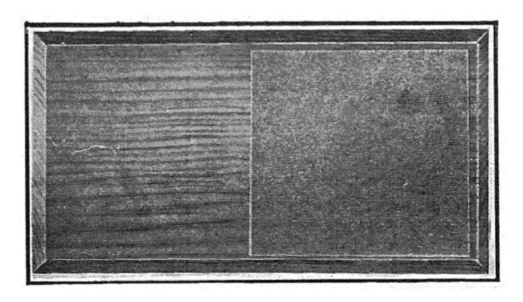

FIG. 13.--BOARD WITH ROUGH AND SMOOTH SURFACES.

During the same period the child can be doing other exercises. Among the material is to be found a small rectangular board, the surface of which is divided into two parts--rough and smooth. (Fig. 13.) The child knows already how to wash his hands with cold water and soap; he then dries them and dips the tips of his fingers for a few seconds in tepid water. Graduated exercises for the thermic sense may also have their place here, as has been explained in my book on the "Method."

After this, the child is taught to pass the soft cushioned tips of his fingers *as lightly as possible* over the two separate surfaces, that he may appreciate their difference. The delicate *movement* backwards and forwards of the suspended hand, as it is brought into light contact with the surface, is an excellent exercise in control. The little hand, which has just been cleansed and given its tepid bath, gains much in grace and beauty, and the whole exercise is the first step in the education of the "tactile sense," which holds such an important place in my method.

When initiating the child into the education of the sense of touch, the teacher must always take an active part the first time; not only must she show the child "how it is done," her interference is a little more definite still, for she takes hold of his hand and guides it to touch the surfaces with the finger-tips in the lightest possible way. She will make no explanations; her words will be rather to *encourage* the child with his hand to perceive the different sensations.

When he has perceived them, it is then that he repeats the act by himself in the delicate way which he has been taught.

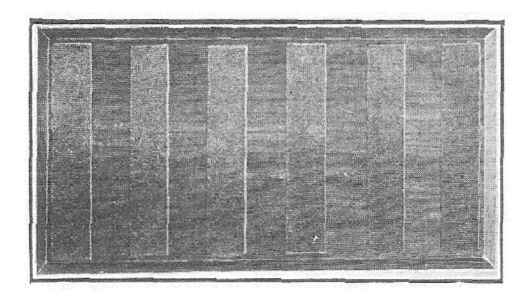

FIG. 14.--BOARD WITH GUMMED STRIPS OF PAPER.

After the board with the two contrasting surfaces, the child is offered another board on which are gummed strips of paper which are rough or smooth in different degrees. (Fig. 14.)

Graduated series of sandpaper cards are also given. The child perfects himself by exercises in touching these surfaces, not only refining his capacity for perceiving tactile differences which are always growing more similar, but also perfecting the movement of which he is ever gaining greater mastery.

Following these is a series of stuffs of every kind: velvets, satins, silks, woolens, cottons, coarse and fine linens. There are two similar pieces of each kind of stuff, and they are of bright and vivid colors.

The child is now taught a new movement. Where before he had to *touch*, he must now *feel* the stuffs, which, according to the degree of fineness or coarseness from coarse cotton to fine silk, are felt with movements correspondingly decisive or delicate. The child whose hand is already practiced finds the greatest pleasure in feeling the stuffs, and, almost instinctively, in order to enhance his appreciation of

[35]

the tactile sensation he closes his eyes. Then, to spare himself the exertion, he blindfolds himself with a clean handkerchief, and as he feels the stuffs, he arranges the similar pieces in pairs, one upon the other, then, taking off the handkerchief, he ascertains for himself whether he has made any mistake.

This exercise in *touching* and *feeling* is peculiarly attractive to the child, and induces him to seek similar experiences in his surroundings. A little one, attracted by the pretty stuff of a visitor's dress, will be seen to go and wash his hands, then to come and touch the stuff of the garment again and again with infinite delicacy, his face meanwhile expressing his pleasure and interest.

* * * * *

A little later we shall see the children interest themselves in a much more difficult exercise.

FIG. 15.--WOOD TABLETS DIFFERING IN WEIGHT.

There are some little rectangular tablets which form part of the material. (Fig. 15.) The tablets, though of identical size, are made of wood of varying qualities, so that they differ in weight and, through the property of the wood, in color also.

The child has to take a tablet and rest it delicately on the inner surfaces of his four fingers, spreading them well out. This will be another opportunity of teaching delicate movements.

The hand must move up and down as though to weigh the object, but the movement must be as imperceptible as possible. These little movements should diminish as the capacity and attention for perceiving the weight of the object becomes more acute and the exercise will be perfectly performed when the child comes to perceive the weight almost without any movement of the hands. It is only by the repetition of the attempts that such a result can be obtained.

Once the children are initiated into it by the teacher, they blindfold their eyes and repeat by themselves these exercises of the *baric sense*. For example, they lay the heavier wooden tablets on the right and the

[36]

lighter on the left.

When the child takes off the handkerchief, he can see by the color of the pieces of wood if he has made a mistake.

* * * * *

A long time before this difficult exercise, and during the period when the child is working with the three sorts of geometrical solids and with the rough and smooth tablets, he can be exercising himself with a material which is very attractive to him.

This is the set of tablets covered with bright silk of shaded colors. The set consists of two separate boxes each containing sixty-four colors; that is, eight different tints, each of which has eight shades carefully graded. The first exercise for the child is that of *pairing the colors*; that is, he selects from a mixed heap of colors the two tablets which are alike, and lays them out, one beside the other. The teacher naturally does not offer the child all the one hundred and twenty-eight tablets in a heap, but chooses only a few of the brighter colors, for example, red, blue and yellow, and prepares and mixes up three or four pairs. Then, taking one tablet--perhaps the red one--she indicates to the child that he is to choose its counterpart from the heap. This done, the teacher lays the pair together on the table. Then she takes perhaps the blue and the child selects the tablet to form another pair. The teacher then mixes the tablets again for the child to repeat the exercise by himself, *i.e.*, to select the two red tablets, the two blue, the two yellow, etc., and to place the two members of each pair next to one another.

Then the couples will be increased to four or five, and little children of three years old end by pairing of their own accord ten or a dozen couples of mixed tablets.

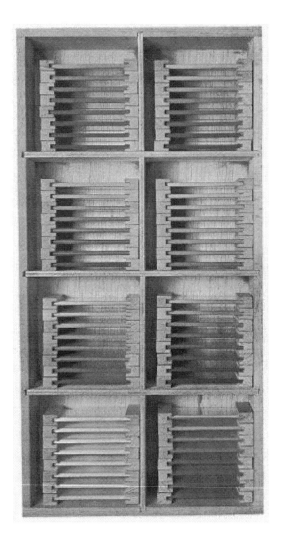

COLOR SPOOLS

When the child has given his eye sufficient practice in recognizing the identity of the pairs of colors, he is offered the shades of one color only, and he exercises himself in the perception of the slightest differences of shade in every color. Take, for example, the blue series. There are eight tablets in graduated shades. The teacher places them one beside another, beginning with the darkest, with the sole object of making the child understand "what is to be done."

She then leaves him alone to the interesting attempts which he spontaneously makes. It often happens that the child makes a mistake. If he has understood the idea and makes a mistake, it is a sign that *he has not yet reached the stage* of perceiving the differences between the graduations of one color. It is practice which perfects in the child that capacity for distinguishing the fine differences, and so we leave him alone to his attempts!

There are two suggestions that we can make to help him. The first is that he should always select the darkest color from the pile. This suggestion greatly facilitates his choice by giving it a constant direction.

Secondly, we can lead him to observe from time to time any two colors that stand next to each other in order to compare them directly and apart from the others. In this way the child does not place a tablet without a particular and careful comparison with its neighbor.

Finally, the child himself will love to mix the sixty-four colors and then to arrange them in eight rows of pretty shades of color with really surprising skill. In this exercise also the child's hand is educated to perform fine and delicate movements and his mind is afforded special training in attention. He must not take hold of the tablets anyhow, he must avoid touching the colored silk, and must handle the tablets instead by the pieces of wood at the top and bottom. To arrange the tablets next to one another in a straight line at exactly the same level, so that the series looks like a beautiful shaded ribbon, is an act which demands a manual skill only obtained after considerable practice.

* * * * *

These exercises of the chromatic sense lead, in the case of the older children, to the development of the "color memory." A child having looked carefully at a color, is then invited to look for its companion in a mixed group of colors, without, of course, keeping the color he has observed under his eye to guide him. It is, therefore, by his memory that he recognizes the color, which he no longer compares with a reality but with an image impressed upon his mind.

The children are very fond of this exercise in "color memory"; it makes a lively digression for them, as they run with the image of a color in their minds and look for its corresponding reality in their surroundings. It is a real triumph for them to identify the idea with the corresponding reality and to *hold in their hands* the proof of the mental power they have acquired.

* * * * *

Another interesting piece of material is a little cabinet containing six drawers placed one above another. When they are opened they display six square wooden "frames" in each. (Fig. 16.)

FIG. 16.--CABINET WITH DRAWERS TO HOLD GEOMETRICAL INSETS.

Almost all the frames have a large geometrical figure inserted in the center, each colored blue and provided with a small button for a handle. Each drawer is lined with blue paper, and when the geometrical figure is removed, the bottom is seen to reproduce exactly the same form.

The geometrical figures are arranged in the drawers according to analogy of form.

(1) In one drawer there are six circles decreasing in diameter. (Fig. 17.)

FIG. 17.--SET OF SIX CIRCLES.

(2) In another there is a square, together with five rectangles in which the length is always equal to the side of the square while the breadth gradually decreases. (Fig. 18.)

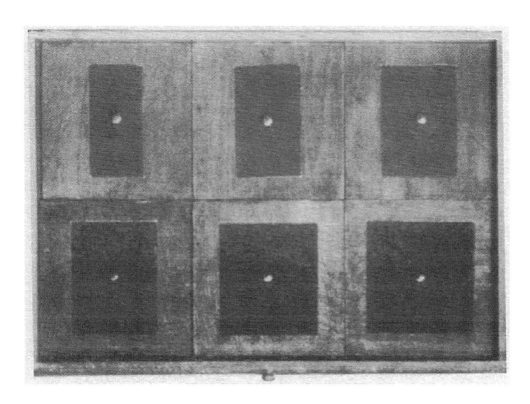

FIG. 18.--SET OF SIX RECTANGLES.

(3) Another drawer contains six triangles, which vary either according to their sides or according to their angles (the equilateral, isosceles, scalene, right angled, obtuse angled, and acute angled). (Fig. 19.)

FIG. 19.--SET OF SIX TRIANGLES

(4) In another drawer there are six regular polygons containing from five to ten sides, *i.e.*, the pentagon, hexagon, heptagon, octagon, nonagon, and decagon. (Fig. 20.)

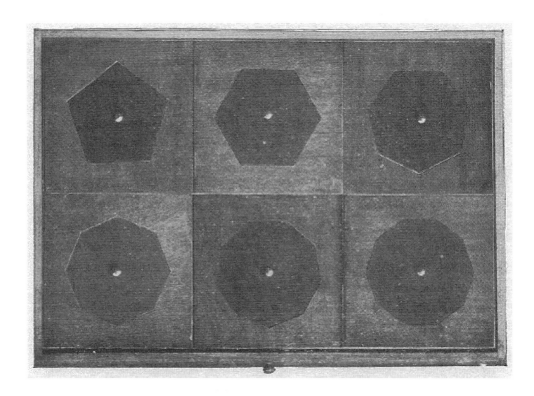

FIG. 20.--SET OF SIX POLYGONS.

(5) Another drawer contains various figures: an oval, an ellipse, a rhombus, and a trapezoid. (Fig. 21.)

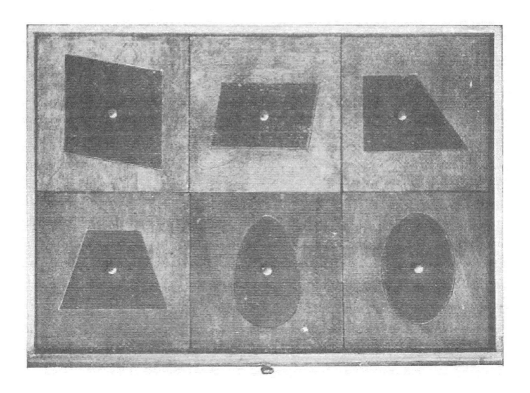

FIG. 21.--SET OF SIX IRREGULAR FIGURES.

(6) Finally, there are four plain wooden tablets, *i.e.*, without any geometrical inset, which should have no button fixed to them; also two other irregular geometrical figures. (Fig. 22.)

FIG. 22.--SET OF FOUR BLANKS AND TWO IRREGULAR FIGURES.

Connected with this material there is a wooden frame furnished with a kind of rack which opens like a lid, and serves, when shut, to keep firmly in place six of the insets which may be arranged on the bottom of the frame itself, entirely covering it. (Fig. 23.)

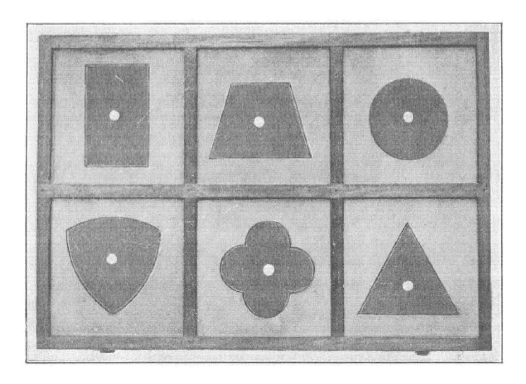

FIG. 23.--FRAME TO HOLD GEOMETRICAL INSETS.

This frame is used for the preparation of the *first presentation* to the child of the plane geometrical forms.

The teacher may select according to her own judgment certain forms from among the whole series at her disposal.

At first it is advisable to show the child only a few figures which differ very widely from one another in form. The next step is to present a larger number of figures, and after this to present consecutively figures more and more similar in form.

The first figures to be arranged in the frame will be, for example, the circle and the equilateral triangle, or the circle, the triangle and the square. The spaces which are left should be covered with the tablets of plain wood. Gradually the frame is completely filled with figures; first, with very dissimilar figures, as, for example, a square, a very narrow rectangle, a triangle, a circle, an ellipse and a hexagon, or with other figures in combination.

Afterwards the teacher's object will be to arrange figures similar to one another in the frame, as, for example, the set of six rectangles, six triangles, six circles, varying in size, etc.

This exercise resembles that of the cylinders. The insets are held by the buttons and taken from their places. They are then mixed on the table and the child is invited to put them back in their places. Here also the control of the error is in the *material*, for the figure cannot be inserted perfectly except when it is put in its own place. Hence a series of "experiments," of "attempts" which end in victory. The child is led to compare the various forms; to realize in a concrete way the differences between them when an inset wrongly placed will not go into the aperture. In this way he educates his eye to the *recognition of forms*.

FIG. 24.--CHILD TOUCHING THE INSETS. (MONTESSORI SCHOOL, RUNTON.)

The new movement of the hand which the child must coordinate is of particular importance. He is taught to *touch the outline of the geometrical figures* with the soft tips of the index and middle finger of the right hand, or of the left as well, if one believes in ambidexterity. (Fig. 24.) The child is made to touch the outline, not only of the *inset*, but also of the corresponding aperture, and, only after *having touched* them, is he to put back the inset into its place.

The *recognition* of the form is rendered much easier in this way. Children who evidently do not *recognize the identities of form* by the eye and who make absurd attempts to place the most diverse figures one within the other, *do recognize* the forms after having touched their outlines, and arrange them very quickly in their right places.

The child's hand during this exercise of touching the outlines of the geometrical figures has a concrete guide in the object. This is especially true when he touches the frames, for his two fingers have only to follow the edge of the frame, which acts as an obstacle and is a very clear guide. The teacher must always intervene at the start to teach accurately this movement, which will have such an importance in the future. She must, therefore, show the child *how to touch*, not only by performing the movement herself slowly and clearly, but also by guiding the child's hand itself during his first attempts, so that he is sure to touch all the details--angles and sides. When his hand has learned to perform these movements with precision and accuracy, he will be *really* capable of following the outline of a geometrical figure, and through many repetitions of the exercise he will come to coordinate the movement *necessary* for the exact delineation of its form.

This exercise could be called an indirect but very real preparation for drawing. It is certainly the preparation of the hand to *trace an enclosed form.* The little hand which touches, feels, and knows how to follow a determined outline is preparing itself, without knowing it, for writing.

The children make a special point of touching the outlines of the plane insets with accuracy. They themselves have invented the exercise of blindfolding their eyes so as to recognize the forms by touch only, taking out and putting back the insets without seeing them.

* * * * *

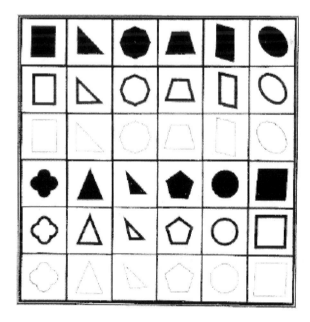

FIG. 25.--SERIES OF CARDS WITH GEOMETRICAL FORMS.

[49]

Corresponding to every form reproduced in the plane insets there are three white cards square in shape and of exactly the same size as the wooden frames of the insets. These cards are kept in three special cardboard boxes, almost cubic in form. (Fig. 25.)

On the cards are repeated, in three series, the same geometrical forms as those of the plane insets. The same measurements of the figures also are exactly reproduced.

In the first series the forms are filled in, *i.e.*, they are cut out in blue paper and gummed on to the card; in the second series there is only an outline about half a centimeter in width, which is cut out in the same blue paper and gummed to the card; in the third series, however, the geometrical figures are instead outlined only in black ink.

By the use of this second piece of the material, the exercise of the eye is gradually brought to perfection in the recognition of "plane forms." In fact, there is no longer the concrete control of error in the material as there was in the *wooden* insets, but the child, by his eye alone, must judge of identities of form when, instead of *fitting* the wooden forms into their corresponding apertures, he simply *rests* them on the cardboard figure.

Again, the refinement of the eye's power of discrimination increases every time the child passes from one series of cards to the next, and by the time that he has reached the third series, he can see the relation between a wooden object, which he holds in his hand, and an outline drawing; that is, he can connect the concrete reality with an *abstraction*. The *line* now assumes in his eyes a very definite meaning; and he accustoms himself to recognize, to interpret and to judge of forms contained by a simple outline.

The exercises are various; the children themselves invent them. Some love to spread out a number of the figures of the geometric insets before their eyes, and then, taking a handful of the cards and mixing them like playing cards, deal them out as quickly as possible, choosing the figures corresponding to the pieces. Then as a test of their choice, they place the wooden pieces upon the forms on the cards. At this exercise they often cover whole tables, putting the wooden figures above, and beneath each one in a vertical line, the three corresponding forms of the cardboard series.

Another game invented by the children consists in putting out and mixing all the cards of the three series on two or three adjoining tables. The child then takes a wooden geometrical form and places it, as quickly as possible, on the corresponding cards which he has recognized at a glance among all the rest.

Four or five children play this game together, and as soon as one of them has found, for example, the filled-in figure corresponding to the wooden piece, and has placed the piece carefully and precisely upon it, another child takes away the piece in order to place it on the same form in outline. The game is somewhat suggestive of chess.

Many children, without any suggestion from any one, touch with the finger the outline of the figures in the three series of cards, doing it with seriousness of purpose, interest and perseverance.

We teach the children to name all the forms of the plane insets.

At first I had intended to limit my teaching to the most important names, such as square, rectangle, circle. But the children wanted to know all the names, taking pleasure in learning even the most difficult, such as trapezium, and decagon. They also show great pleasure in listening to the exact pronunciation of new words and in their repetition. Early childhood is, in fact, the age in which language is formed, and in which the sounds of a foreign language can be perfectly learned.

When the child has had long practice with the plane insets, he begins to make "discoveries" in his environment, recognizing forms, colors, and qualities already known to him--a result which, in general, follows after all the sensory exercises. Then it is that a great enthusiasm is aroused in him, and the world becomes for him a source of pleasure. A little boy, walking one day alone on the roof terrace, repeated to himself with a thoughtful expression on his face, "The sky is blue! the sky is blue!" Once a cardinal, an admirer of the children of the school in Via Guisti, wished himself to bring them some biscuits and to enjoy the sight of a little greediness among the children. When he had finished his distribution, instead of seeing the children put the food hastily into their mouths, to his great surprise he heard them call out, "A triangle! a circle! a rectangle!" In fact, these biscuits were made in geometrical shapes.

In one of the people's dwellings at Milan, a mother, preparing the dinner in the kitchen, took from a packet a slice of bread and butter. Her little four-year-old boy who was with her said, "Rectangle." The woman going on with her work cut off a large corner of the slice of bread, and the child cried out, "Triangle." She put this bit into the saucepan, and the child, looking at the piece that was left, called out more loudly than before, "And now it is a trapezium."

The father, a working man, who was present, was much impressed with the incident. He went straight to look for the teacher and asked for an explanation. Much moved, he said, "If I had been educated in that way I should not be now just an ordinary workman."

It was he who later on arranged for a demonstration to induce all the workmen of the dwellings to take an interest in the school. They ended by presenting the teacher with a parchment they had painted themselves, and on it, between the pictures of little children, they had introduced every kind of geometrical form.

As regards the touching of objects for the realization of their form, there is an infinite field of discovery open to the child in his environment. Children have been seen to stand opposite a beautiful pillar or a statue and, after having admired it, to close their eyes in a state of beatitude and pass their hands many times over the forms. One of our teachers met one day in a church two little brothers from the school in Via Guisti. They were standing looking at the small columns supporting the altar. Little by little the elder boy edged nearer the columns and began to touch them, then, as if he desired his little brother to share his pleasure, he drew him nearer and, taking his hand very gently, made him pass it round the smooth and beautiful shape of the column. But a sacristan came up at that moment and sent away "those tiresome children who were touching everything."

The great pleasure which the children derive from the recognition of *objects* by touching their form corresponds in itself to a sensory exercise.

Many psychologists have spoken of the *stereognostic* sense, that is, the capacity of recognizing forms by the movement of the muscles of the hand as it follows the outlines of solid objects. This sense does not consist only of the sense of touch, because the tactile sensation is only that by which we perceive the differences in quality of surfaces, rough or smooth. Perception of form comes from the combination of two sensations, tactile and muscular, muscular sensations being sensations of movement. What we call in the blind the *tactile* sense is in reality more often the stereognostic sense. That is, they perceive by means of their hands the *form of bodies*.

It is the special muscular sensibility of the child from three to six years of age who is forming his own muscular activity which stimulates him to use the stereognostic sense. When the child spontaneously blindfolds his eyes in order to recognize various objects, such as the plane and solid insets, he is exercising this sense.

There are many exercises which he can do to enable him to recognize with closed eyes objects of well defined shapes, as, for example, the little bricks and cubes of Froebel, marbles, coins, beans, peas, etc. From a selection of different objects mixed together he can pick out those that are alike, and arrange them in separate heaps.

In the didactic material there are also geometrical solids--pale blue in color--a sphere, a prism, a pyramid, a cone, a cylinder. The most attractive way of teaching a child to recognize these forms is for him to touch them with closed eyes and guess their names, the latter learned in a way which I will describe later. After an exercise of this kind the child when his eyes are open observes the forms with a much more lively interest. Another way of interesting him in the solid geometrical forms is to make them *move*. The sphere rolls in every direction; the cylinder rolls in one direction only; the cone rolls round itself; the prism and the pyramid, however, stand still, but the prism falls over more easily than the pyramid.

* * * * *

FIG. 26.--SOUND BOXES.

Little more remains of the didactic material for the education of the senses. There is, however, a series of six cardboard cylinders, either closed entirely or with wooden covers. (Fig. 26.)

When these cases are shaken they produce sounds varying in intensity from loud to almost imperceptible sounds, according to the nature of the objects inside the cylinder.

There is a double act of these, and the exercise consists, first, in the recognition of sounds of equal intensity, arranging the cylinders in pairs. The next exercise consists in the comparison of one sound with another; that is, the child arranges the six cylinders in a series according to the loudness of sound which they produce. The exercise is analogous to that with the color spools, which also are paired and then arranged in gradation. In this case also the child performs the exercise seated comfortably at a table. After a preliminary explanation from the teacher he repeats the exercise by himself, his eyes being blindfolded that he may better concentrate his attention.

We may conclude with a general rule for the direction of the education of the senses. The order of procedure should be:

(1) Recognition of *identities* (the pairing of similar objects and the insertion of solid forms into places which fit them).

(2) Recognition of *contrasts* (the presentation of the extremes of a series of objects).

(3) Discrimination between objects very *similar* to one another.

To concentrate the attention of the child upon the sensory stimulus which is acting upon him at a particular moment, it is well, as far as possible, to *isolate* the sense; for instance, to obtain silence in the room for all the exercises and to blindfold the eyes for those particular exercises which do not relate to the education of the sense of sight.

The cinematograph pictures give a general idea of all the sense exercises which the children can do with the material, and any one who has been initiated into the theory on which these are based will be able gradually to recognize them as they are seen practically carried out.

It is very advisable for those who wish to guide the children in these sensory exercises to begin themselves by working with the didactic material. The experience will give them some idea of what the children must feel, of the difficulties which they must overcome, etc., and, up to a certain point, it will give them some conception of the interest which these exercises can arouse in them. Whoever makes such experiments himself will be most struck by the fact that, when blindfolded, he finds that all the sensations of touch and hearing really appear more acute and more easily recognized. On account of this alone no small interest will be aroused in the experimenter.

* * * * *

For the beginning of the education of the musical sense, we use in Rome a material which does not form part of the didactic apparatus as it is sold at present. It consists of a double series of bells forming an octave with tones and semitones. These metal bells, which stand upon a wooden rectangular base, are all alike in appearance, but, when struck with a little wooden hammer, give out sounds corresponding to the notes doh, re, mi, fah, soh, lah, ti, doh, doh [sharp], re [sharp], fah [sharp], soh [sharp], lah [sharp].

Musical Scale (Chromatic)

FIG. 27.--MUSICAL BELLS.

One series of bells is arranged in chromatic order upon a long board, upon which are painted rectangular spaces which are black and white and of the same size as the bases which support the bells. As on a pianoforte keyboard, the white spaces correspond to the tones, and the black to the semitones. (Fig. 27.)

At first the only bells to be arranged upon the board are those which correspond to the tones; these are set upon the white spaces in the order of the musical notes, doh, re, mi, fah, soh, lah, ti, doh.

To perform the first exercise the child strikes with a small hammer the first note of the series already arranged (doh). Then among a second series of corresponding bells which, arranged without the semitones, are mixed together upon the table, he tries, by striking the bells one after the other, to find the sound which is the same as the first one he has struck (doh). When he has succeeded in finding the corresponding sound, he puts the bell thus chosen opposite the first one (doh) upon the board. Then he strikes the second bell, *re*, once or twice; then from among the mixed group of bells he makes experiments until he recognizes *re*, which he places opposite the second bell of the series already arranged. He continues in the same way right to the end, looking for the identity of the sounds and performing an exercise of *pairing* similar to that already done in the case of the sound-boxes, the colors, etc.

Later, he learns in order the sounds of the musical scale, striking in rapid succession the bells arranged in order, and also accompanying his action with his voice--doh, re, mi, fah, soh, lah, ti, doh. When he is able to recognize and *remember* the series of sounds, the child takes the eight bells and, after mixing them up, he tries by striking them with the hammer, to find *doh*, then *re*, etc. Every time that he takes a new note, he strikes from the beginning all the bells already recognized and arranged in order--doh, *re*, doh, re, *mi*; doh, re, mi, *fah*; doh, re, mi, fah, *soh*, etc. In this way he succeeds in arranging all the bells in the order of the scale, guided only by his ear, and having succeeded, he strikes all the notes one after the other up and down the scale. This exercise fascinates children from five years old upwards.

If the objects which have been described constitute the didactic material for the beginnings of a methodical education of the auditory sense, I have no desire to limit to them an educational process which is so important and already so complex in its practice, whether in the long established methods of treatment for the deaf, or in modern physiological musical education. In fact, I also use resonant metal tubes, small bars of wood which emit musical notes, and strings (little harps), upon which the children seek to recognize the tones they have already learned with the exercise of the bells. The pianoforte may also be used for the same purpose. In this way the difference in *timbre* comes to be perceived together with the differences in tone. At the same time various exercises, already mentioned, such as the marches played on the piano for rhythmic exercises, and the simple songs sung by the children themselves, offer extensive means for the development of the musical sense.

* * * * *

To quicken the child's attention in special relation to sounds there is a most important exercise which, contrary to all attempts made up to this time in the practice of education, consists not in producing but in eliminating, as far as possible, all sounds from the environment. My "lesson of silence" has been very widely applied, even in schools where the rest of my method has not found its way, for the sake of its practical effect upon the discipline of the children.

The children are taught "not to move"; to inhibit all those motor impulses which may arise from any cause whatsoever, and in order to induce in them real "immobility," it is necessary to initiate them in the *control* of all their movements. The teacher, then, does not limit herself to saying, "Sit still," but she gives them the example herself, showing them how to sit absolutely still; that is, with feet still, body still, arms still, head still. The respiratory movements should also be performed in such a way as to produce no sound.

The children must be taught how to succeed in this exercise. The fundamental condition is that of finding a comfortable position, *i.e.*, a position of equilibrium. As they are seated for this exercise, they must therefore make themselves comfortable either in their little chairs or on the ground. When immobility is obtained, the room is half-darkened, or else the children close their eyes, or cover them with their hands.

It is quite plain to see that the children take a great interest in the "Silence"; they seem to give themselves up to a kind of spell: they might be said to be wrapped in meditation. Little by little, as each child, watching himself, becomes more and more still, the silence deepens till it becomes absolute and can be felt, just as the twilight gradually deepens whilst the sun is setting.

Then it is that slight sounds, unnoticed before, are heard; the ticking of the clock, the chirp of a sparrow in the garden, the flight of a butterfly. The world becomes full of imperceptible sounds which invade that deep silence without disturbing it, just as the stars shine out in the dark sky without banishing the darkness of the night. It is almost the discovery of a new world where there is rest. It is, as it were, the twilight of the world of loud noises and of the uproar that oppresses the spirit. At such a time the spirit is set free and opens out like the corolla of the convolvulus.

And leaving metaphor for the reality of facts, can we not all recall feelings that have possessed us at sunset, when all the vivid impressions of the day, the brightness and clamor, are silenced? It is not that we miss the day, but that our spirit expands. It becomes more sensitive to the inner play of emotions, strong and persistent, or changeful and serene.

"It was that hour when mariners feel longing, And hearts grow tender."

(Dante, trans. Longfellow.)

The lesson of silence ends with a general calling of the children's names. The teacher, or one of the children, takes her place behind the class or in an adjoining room, and "calls" the motionless children, one by one, by name; the call is made in a whisper, that is, without vocal sound. This demands a close attention on the part of the child, if he is to hear his name. When his name is called he must rise and find his way to the voice which called him; his movements must be light and vigilant, and so controlled *as to make no noise.*

When the children have become acquainted with *silence*, their hearing is in a manner refined for the perception of sounds. Those sounds which are too loud become gradually displeasing to the ear of one who has known the pleasure of silence, and has discovered the world of delicate sounds. From this point the children gradually go on to perfect themselves; they walk lightly, take care not to knock against the furniture, move their chairs without noise, and place things upon the table with great care. The result of this is seen in the grace of carriage and of movement, which is especially delightful on account of the way in which it has been brought about. It is not a grace taught externally for the sake of beauty or regard for the world, but one which is born of the pleasure felt by the spirit in immobility and silence. The soul of the child wishes to free itself from the irksomeness of sounds that are too loud, from obstacles to its peace during work. These children, with the grace of pages to a noble lord, are serving their spirits.

This exercise develops very definitely the social spirit. No other lesson, no other "situation," could do the same. A profound silence can be obtained even when more than fifty children are crowded together in a small space, provided that *all* the children know how to keep still and want to do it; but one disturber is enough to take away the charm.

[57]

Here is demonstration of the cooperation of all the members of a community to achieve a common end. The children gradually show increased power of *inhibition*; many of them, rather than disturb the silence, refrain from brushing a fly off the nose, or suppress a cough or sneeze. The same exhibition of collective action is seen in the care with which the children move to avoid making a noise during their work. The lightness with which they run on tiptoe, the grace with which they shut a cupboard, or lay an object on the table, these are qualities that must be *acquired by all*, if the environment is to become tranquil and free from disturbance. One rebel is sufficient to mar this achievement; one noisy child, walking on his heels or banging the door, can disturb the peaceful atmosphere of the small community.

Language and Knowledge of the World

The special importance of the sense of hearing comes from the fact that it is the sense organ connected with speech. Therefore, to train the child's attention to follow sounds and noises which are produced in the environment, to recognize them and to discriminate between them, is to prepare his attention to follow more accurately the sounds of articulate language. The teacher must be careful to pronounce clearly and completely the sounds of the word when she speaks to a child, even though she may be speaking in a low voice, almost as if telling him a secret. The children's songs are also a good means for obtaining exact pronunciation. The teacher, when she teaches them, pronounces slowly, separating the component sounds of the word pronounced.

But a special opportunity for training in clear and exact speech occurs when the lessons are given in the nomenclature relating to the sensory exercises. In every exercise, when the child has *recognized* the differences between the qualities of the objects, the teacher fixes the idea of this quality with a word. Thus, when the child has many times built and rebuilt the tower of the pink cubes, at an opportune moment the teacher draws near him, and taking the two extreme cubes, the largest and the smallest, and showing them to him, says, "This is large"; "This is small." The two words only, *large* and *small*, are pronounced several times in succession with strong emphasis and with a very clear pronunciation, "This is *large*, large, large"; after which there is a moment's pause. Then the teacher, to see if the child has understood, verifies with the following tests: "Give me the large one. Give me the *small* one." Again, "The large one." "Now the small one." "Give me the large one." Then there is another pause. Finally, the teacher, pointing to the objects in turn asks, "What is this?" The child, if he has learned, replies rightly, "Large," "Small." The teacher then urges the child to repeat the words always more clearly and as accurately as possible. "What is it?" "Large." "What?" "Large." "Tell me nicely, what is it?" "Large."

Large and *small* objects are those which differ only in size and not in form; that is, all three dimensions change more or less proportionally. We should say that a house is "large" and a hut is "small." When two pictures represent the same objects in different dimensions one can be said to be an enlargement of the other.

When, however, only the dimensions referring to the section of the object change, while the length remains the same, the objects are respectively "thick" and "thin." We should say of two posts of equal height, but different cross-section, that one is "thick" and the other is "thin." The teacher, therefore, gives a lesson on the brown prisms similar to that with the cubes in the three "periods" which I have described:

Period 1. Naming. "This is thick. This is thin."

Period 2. Recognition. "Give me the *thick*. Give me the *thin*."

Period 3. The Pronunciation of the Word. "What is this?"

There is a way of helping the child to recognize differences in dimension and to place the objects in correct gradation. After the lesson which I have described, the teacher scatters the brown prisms, for instance, on a carpet, says to the child, "Give me the thickest of all," and lays the object on a table. Then, again, she invites the child to look for *the thickest* piece among those scattered on the floor, and every time the piece chosen is laid in its order on the table next to the piece previously chosen. In this way the child accustoms himself always to look either for the *thickest* or the *thinnest* among the rest, and so has a guide to help him to lay the pieces in gradation.

When there is one dimension only which varies, as in the case of the rods, the objects are said to be "long" and "short," the varying dimension being length. When the varying dimension is height, the objects are said to be "tall" and "short"; when the breadth varies, they are "broad" and "narrow."

Of these three varieties we offer the child as a fundamental lesson only that in which the *length* varies, and we teach the differences by means of the usual "three periods," and by asking him to select from the pile at one time always the "longest," at another always the "shortest."

The child in this way acquires great accuracy in the use of words. One day the teacher had ruled the blackboard with very fine lines. A child said, "What small lines!" "They are not small," corrected another; "they are *thin*."

When the names to be taught are those of colors or of forms, so that it is not necessary to emphasize contrast between extremes, the teacher can give more than two names at the same time, as, for instance, "This is red." "This is blue." "This is yellow." Or, again, "This is a square." "This is a triangle." "This is a circle." In the case of a *gradation*, however, the teacher will select (if she is teaching the colors) the two extremes "dark" and "light," then making choice always of the "darkest" and the "lightest."

Many of the lessons here described can be seen in the cinematograph pictures; lessons on touching the plane insets and the surfaces, in walking on the line, in color memory, in the nomenclature relating to the cubes and the long rods, in the composition of words, reading, writing, etc.

By means of these lessons the child comes to know many words very thoroughly--large, small; thick, thin; long, short; dark, light; rough, smooth; heavy, light; hot, cold; and the names of many colors and geometrical forms. Such words do not relate to any particular *object*, but to a psychic acquisition on the part of the child. In fact, the name is given *after a long exercise*, in which the child, concentrating his attention on different qualities of objects, has made comparisons, reasoned, and formed judgments,

[60]

until he has acquired a power of discrimination which he did not possess before. In a word, he has *refined his senses*; his observation of things has been thorough and fundamental; he has *changed himself.*

He finds himself, therefore, facing the world with *psychic* qualities refined and quickened. His powers of observation and of recognition have greatly increased. Further, the mental images which he has succeeded in establishing are not a confused medley; they are all classified--forms are distinct from dimensions, and dimensions are classed according to the qualities which result from the combinations of varying dimensions.

All these are quite distinct from *gradations*. Colors are divided according to tint and to richness of tone, silence is distinct from non-silence, noises from sounds, and everything has its own exact and appropriate name. The child then has not only developed in himself special qualities of observation and of judgment, but the objects which he observes may be said to go into their place, according to the order established in his mind, and they are placed under their appropriate name in an exact classification.

Does not the student of the experimental sciences prepare himself in the same way to observe the outside world? He may find himself like the uneducated man in the midst of the most diverse natural objects, but he differs from the uneducated man in that he has *special qualities* for observation. If he is a worker with the microscope, his eyes are trained to see in the range of the microscope certain minute details which the ordinary man cannot distinguish. If he is an astronomer, he will look through the same telescope as the curious visitor or *dilettante*, but he will see much more clearly. The same plants surround the botanist and the ordinary wayfarer, but the botanist sees in every plant those qualities which are classified in his mind, and assigns to each plant its own place in the natural orders, giving it its exact name. It is this capacity for recognizing a plant in a complex order of classification which distinguishes the botanist from the ordinary gardener, and it is *exact* and scientific language which characterizes the trained observer.

Now, the scientist who has developed special qualities of observation and who "possesses" an order in which to classify external objects will be the man to make scientific *discoveries*. It will never be he who, without preparation and order, wanders dreaming among plants or beneath the starlit sky.

In fact, our little ones have the impression of continually "making discoveries" in the world about them; and in this they find the greatest joy. They take from the world a knowledge which is ordered and inspires them with enthusiasm. Into their minds there enters "the Creation" instead of "the Chaos"; and it seems that their souls find therein a divine exultation.

Freedom

The success of these results is closely connected with the delicate intervention of the one who guides the children in their development. It is necessary for the teacher to *guide* the child without letting him feel her presence too much, so that she may be always ready to supply the desired help, but may never be the obstacle between the child and his experience.

A lesson in the ordinary use of the word cools the child's enthusiasm for the knowledge of things, just as it would cool the enthusiasm of adults. To keep alive that enthusiasm is the secret of real guidance, and it will not prove a difficult task, provided that the attitude towards the child's acts be that of respect, calm and waiting, and provided that he be left free in his movements and in his experiences.

Then we shall notice that the child has a personality which he is seeking to expand; he has initiative, he chooses his own work, persists in it, changes it according to his inner needs; he does not shirk effort, he rather goes in search of it, and with great joy overcomes obstacles within his capacity. He is sociable to the extent of wanting to share with every one his successes, his discoveries, and his little triumphs. There is therefore no need of intervention. "Wait while observing." That is the motto for the educator.

Let us wait, and be always ready to share in both the joys and the difficulties which the child experiences. He himself invites our sympathy, and we should respond fully and gladly. Let us have endless patience with his slow progress, and show enthusiasm and gladness at his successes. If we could say: "We are respectful and courteous in our dealings with children, we treat them as we should like to be treated ourselves," we should certainly have mastered a great educational principle and undoubtedly be setting an *example of good education.*

What we all desire for ourselves, namely, not to be disturbed in our work, not to find hindrances to our efforts, to have good friends ready to help us in times of need, to see them rejoice with us, to be on terms of equality with them, to be able to confide and trust in them--this is what we need for happy companionship. In the same way children are human beings to whom respect is due, superior to us by reason of their "innocence" and of the greater possibilities of their future. What we desire they desire also.

As a rule, however, we do not respect our children. We try to force them to follow us without regard to their special needs. We are overbearing with them, and above all, rude; and then we expect them to be submissive and well-behaved, knowing all the time how strong is their instinct of imitation and how touching their faith in and admiration of us. They will imitate us in any case. Let us treat them, therefore, with all the kindness which we would wish to help to develop in them. And by kindness is not meant caresses. Should we not call anyone who embraced us at the first time of meeting rude, vulgar and ill-bred? Kindness consists in interpreting the wishes of others, in conforming one's self to them, and sacrificing, if need be, one's own desire. This is the kindness which we must show towards children.

To find the interpretation of children's desires we must study them scientifically, for their desires are often unconscious. They are the inner cry of life, which wishes to unfold according to mysterious laws. We know very little of the way in which it unfolds. Certainly the child is growing into a man by force of a divine action similar to that by which from nothing he became a child.

Our intervention in this marvelous process is *indirect*; we are here to offer to this life, which came into the world by itself, the *means* necessary for its development, and having done that we must await this development with respect.

Let us leave the life *free* to develop within the limits of the good, and let us observe this inner life developing. This is the whole of our mission. Perhaps as we watch we shall be reminded of the words of Him who was absolutely good, "Suffer the little children to come unto Me." That is to say, "Do not hinder them from coming, since, if they are left free and unhampered, they will come."

 Writing

The child who has completed all the exercises above described, and is thus *prepared* for an advance towards unexpected conquests, is about four years old.

He is not an unknown quantity, as are children who have been left to gain varied and casual experiences by themselves, and who therefore differ in type and intellectual standard, not only according to their "natures," but especially according to the chances and opportunities they have found for their spontaneous inner formation.

Education has *determined an environment* for the children. Individual differences to be found in them can, therefore, be put down almost exclusively to each one's individual "nature." Owing to their environment which offers *means* adapted and measured to meet the needs of their psychical development, our children have acquired a fundamental type which is common to all. They have *coordinated* their movements in various kinds of manual work about the house, and so have acquired a characteristic independence of action, and initiative in the adaptation of their actions to their environment. Out of all this emerges a *personality*, for the children have become little men, who are self-reliant.

The special attention necessary to handle small fragile objects without breaking them, and to move heavy articles without making a noise, has endowed the movements of the whole body with a lightness and grace which are characteristic of our children. It is a deep feeling of responsibility which has brought them to such a pitch of perfection. For instance, when they carry three or four tumblers at a time, or a tureen of hot soup, they know that they are responsible not only for the objects, but also for the success of the meal which at that moment they are directing. In the same way each child feels the responsibility of the "silence," of the prevention of harsh sounds, and he knows how to cooperate for the general good in keeping the environment, not only orderly, but quiet and calm. Indeed, our children have taken the road which leads them to mastery of themselves.

But their formation is due to a deeper psychological work still, arising from the education of the senses. In addition to ordering their environment and ordering themselves in their outward personalities, they have also ordered the inner world of their minds.

The didactic material, in fact, does not offer to the child the "content" of the mind, but the *order* for that "content." It causes him to distinguish identities from differences, extreme differences from fine gradations, and to classify, under conceptions of quality and of quantity, the most varying sensations appertaining to surfaces, colors, dimensions, forms and sounds. The mind has formed itself by a special exercise of attention, observing, comparing, and classifying.

The mental attitude acquired by such an exercise leads the child to make ordered observations in his environment, observations which prove as interesting to him as discoveries, and so stimulate him to multiply them indefinitely and to form in his mind a rich "content" of clear ideas.

Language now comes to *fix* by means of *exact words* the ideas which the mind has acquired. These words are few in number and have reference, not to separate objects, but rather to the *order of the ideas* which have been formed in the mind. In this way the children are able to "find themselves," alike in the world of natural things and in the world of objects and of words which surround them, for they have an inner guide which leads them to become *active and intelligent explorers* instead of wandering wayfarers in an unknown land.

These are the children who, in a short space of time, sometimes in a few days, learn to write and to perform the first operations of arithmetic. It is not a fact that children in general can do it, as many have believed. It is not a case of giving my material for writing to unprepared children and of awaiting the "miracle."

The fact is that the minds and hands of our children are already *prepared* for writing, and ideas of quantity, of identity, of differences, and of gradation, which form the bases of all calculation, have been maturing for a long time in them.

One might say that all their previous education is a preparation for the first stages of essential culture--*writing, reading, and number,* and that knowledge comes as an easy, spontaneous, and logical consequence of the preparation--that it is in fact its natural *conclusion.*

We have already seen that the purpose of the *word* is to fix ideas and to facilitate the elementary comprehension of *things.* In the same way writing and arithmetic now fix the complex inner acquisitions of the mind, which proceeds henceforward continually to enrich itself by fresh observations.

* * * * *

Our children have long been preparing the hand for writing. Throughout all the sensory exercises the hand, whilst cooperating with the mind in its attainments and in its work of formation, was preparing its own future. When the hand learned to hold itself lightly suspended over a horizontal surface in order to touch rough and smooth, when it took the cylinders of the solid insets and placed them in their apertures, when with two fingers it touched the outlines of the geometrical forms, it was coordinating movements, and the child is now ready--almost impatient to use them in the fascinating "synthesis" of writing.

The *direct* preparation for writing also consists in exercises of the movements of the hand. There are two series of exercises, very different from one another. I have analyzed the movements which are connected with writing, and I prepare them separately one from the other. When we write, we perform a movement for the *management* of the instrument of writing, a movement which generally acquires an individual character, so that a person's handwriting can be recognized, and, in certain medical cases, changes in the nervous system can be traced by the corresponding alterations in the handwriting. In fact, it is from the handwriting that specialists in that subject would interpret the *moral character* of individuals.

Writing has, besides this, a general character, which has reference to the form of the alphabetical signs.

When a man writes he combines these two parts, but they actually exist as the *component parts of a single product* and can be prepared apart.

Exercises for the Management of the Instrument of Writing

(THE INDIVIDUAL PART)

In the didactic material there are two sloping wooden boards, on each of which stand five square metal frames, colored pink. In each of these is inserted a blue geometrical figure similar to the geometrical insets and provided with a small button for a handle. With this material we use a box of ten colored pencils and a little book of designs which I have prepared after five years' experience of observing the children. I have chosen and graduated the designs according to the use which the children made of them.

The two sloping boards are set side by side, and on them are placed ten complete "insets," that is to say, the frames with the geometrical figures. (Fig. 28.) The child is given a sheet of white paper and the box of ten colored pencils. He will then choose one of the ten metal insets, which are arranged in an attractive line at a certain distance from him. The child is taught the following process:

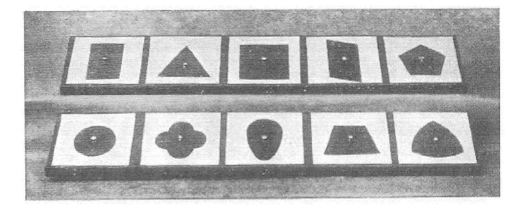

FIG. 28.--SLOPING BOARDS TO DISPLAY SET OF METAL INSETS.

He lays the frame of the iron inset on the sheet of paper, and, holding it down firmly with one hand, he follows with a colored pencil the interior outline which describes a geometrical figure. Then he lifts the square frame, and finds drawn upon the paper an enclosed geometrical form, a triangle, a circle, a hexagon, etc. The child has not actually performed a new exercise, because he had already performed all these movements when he *touched* the wooden plane insets. The only new feature of the exercise is that he follows the outlines no longer directly with his finger, but through the medium of a pencil. That is, he *draws, he leaves a trace* of his movement.

The child finds this exercise easy and most interesting, and, as soon as he has succeeded in making the first outline, he places above it the piece of blue metal corresponding to it. This is an exercise exactly similar to that which he performed when he placed the wooden geometrical figures upon the cards of the third series, where the figures are only contained by a simple line.

This time, however, when the action of placing the form upon the outline is performed, the child takes *another colored pencil* and draws the outline of the blue metal figure.

When he raises it, if the drawing is well done, he finds upon the paper a geometrical figure contained by two outlines in colors, and, if the colors have been well chosen, the result is very attractive, and the child, who has already had a considerable education of the chromatic sense is keenly interested in it.

These may seem unnecessary details, but, as a matter of fact, they are all-important. For instance, if, instead of arranging the ten metal insets in a row, the teacher distributes them among the children without thus exhibiting them, the child's exercises are much limited. When, on the other hand, the insets are exhibited before his eyes, he feels the desire to draw them *all* one after the other, and the number of exercises is increased.

The two *colored outlines* rouse the desire of the child to see another combination of colors and then to repeat the experience. The variety of the objects and the colors are therefore an *inducement* to work and hence to final success.

Here the actual preparatory movement for writing begins. When the child has drawn the figure in double outline, he takes hold of a pencil "like a pen for writing," and draws marks up and down until he has completely filled the figure. In this way a definite filled-in figure remains on the paper, similar to the figures on the cards of the first series. This figure can be in any of the ten colors. At first the children fill in the figures very clumsily without regard for the outlines, making very heavy lines and not keeping them parallel. Little by little, however, the drawings improve, in that they keep within the outlines, and the lines increase in number, grow finer, and are parallel to one another.

When the child has begun these exercises, he is seized with a desire to continue them, and he never tires of drawing the outlines of the figures and then filling them in. Each child suddenly becomes the possessor of a considerable number of drawings, and he treasures them up in his own little drawer. In this way he *organizes* the movement of writing, which brings him *to the management of the pen.* This movement in ordinary methods is represented by the wearisome pothook connected with the first laborious and tedious attempts at writing.

The organization of this movement, which began from the guidance of a piece of metal, is as yet rough and imperfect, and the child now passes on to the *filling in of the prepared designs* in the little album. The leaves are taken from the book one by one in the order of progression in which they are arranged, and the child fills in the prepared designs with colored pencils in the same way as before. Here the choice of the colors is another intelligent occupation which encourages the child to multiply the tasks. He chooses the colors by himself and with much taste. The delicacy of the shades which he chooses and the harmony with which he arranges them in these designs show us that the common belief, that children love *bright and glaring* colors, has been the result of observation of *children without education,* who have been abandoned to the rough and harsh experiences of an environment unfitted for them.

The education of the chromatic sense becomes at this point of a child's development the *lever* which enables him to become possessed of a firm, bold and beautiful handwriting.

The drawings lend themselves to *limiting,* in very many ways, *the length of the strokes with which they are filled in.* The child will have to fill in geometrical figures, both large and small, of a pavement design, or flowers and leaves, or the various details of an animal or of a landscape. In this way the hand accustoms itself, not only to perform the general action, but also to confine the movement within all kinds of limits.

Hence the child is preparing himself to write in a handwriting *either* large or small. Indeed, later on he will write as well between the wide lines on a blackboard as between the narrow, closely ruled lines of an exercise book, generally used by much older children.

The number of exercises which the child performs with the drawings is practically unlimited. He will often take another colored pencil and draw over again the outlines of the figure already filled in with color. A help to the *continuation* of the exercise is to be found in the further education of the chromatic sense, which the child acquires by painting the same designs in water-colors. Later he mixes colors for himself until he can imitate the colors of nature, or create the delicate tints which his own imagination desires. It is not possible, however, to speak of all this in detail within the limits of this small work.

Exercises for the Writing of Alphabetical Signs

FIG. 29.--SINGLE SANDPAPER LETTER.

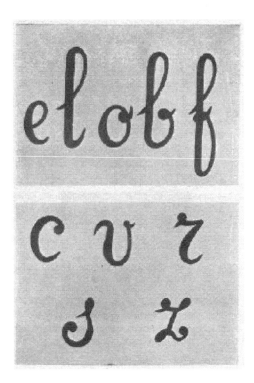

FIG. 30.--GROUPS OF SANDPAPER LETTERS.

In the didactic material there are series of boxes which contain the alphabetical signs. At this point we take those cards which are covered with very smooth paper, to which is gummed a letter of the alphabet cut out in sandpaper. (Fig. 29.) There are also large cards on which are gummed several letters, grouped together according to analogy of form. (Fig. 30.)

[70]

The children "have to *touch* over the alphabetical signs as though they were writing." They touch them with the tips of the index and middle fingers in the same way as when they touched the wooden insets, and with the hand raised as when they lightly touched the rough and smooth surfaces. The teacher herself touches the letters to show the child how the movement should be performed, and the child, if he has had much practice in touching the wooden insets, *imitates* her with *ease* and pleasure. Without the previous practice, however, the child's hand does not follow the letter with accuracy, and it is most interesting to make close observations of the children in order to understand the importance of a *remote motor preparation* for writing, and also to realize the *immense* strain which we impose upon the children when we set them to write directly without a previous motor education of the hand.

The child finds great pleasure in touching the sandpaper letters. It is an exercise by which he applies to a new attainment the power he has already acquired through exercising the sense of touch. Whilst the child touches a letter, the teacher pronounces its sound, and she uses for the lesson the usual three periods. Thus, for example, presenting the two vowels *i, o,* she will have the child touch them slowly and accurately, and repeat their relative sounds one after the other as the child touches them, "i, i, i! o, o, o!" Then she will say to the child: "Give me i!" "Give me o!" Finally, she will ask the question: "What is this?" To which the child replies, "i, o." She proceeds in the same way through all the other letters, giving, in the case of the consonants, not the name, but only the sound. The child then touches the letters by himself over and over again, either on the separate cards or on the large cards on which several letters are gummed, and in this way he establishes the movements necessary for tracing the alphabetical signs. At the same time he retains the *visual* image of the letter. This process forms the first preparation, not only for writing, but also for reading, because it is evident that when the child *touches* the letters he performs the movement corresponding to the writing of them, and, at the same time, when he recognizes them by sight he is reading the alphabet.

The child has thus prepared, in effect, all the necessary movements for writing; therefore he *can write*. This important conquest is the result of a long period of inner formation of which the child is not clearly aware. But a day will come--very soon--when he *will write*, and that will be a day of great surprise for him--the wonderful harvest of an unknown sowing.

* * * * *

FIG. 31.--BOX OF MOVABLE LETTERS.

The alphabet of movable letters cut out in pink and blue cardboard, and kept in a special box with compartments, serves "for the composition of words." (Fig. 31.)

In a phonetic language, like Italian, it is enough to pronounce clearly the different component sounds of a word (as, for example, m-a-n-o), so that the child whose ear is *already educated* may recognize one by one the component sounds. Then he looks in the movable alphabet for the *signs* corresponding to each separate sound, and lays them one beside the other, thus composing the word (for instance, mano). Gradually he will become able to do the same thing with words of which he thinks himself; he succeeds in breaking them up into their component sounds, and in translating them into a row of signs.

When the child has composed the words in this way, he knows how to read them. In this method, therefore, all the processes leading to writing include reading as well.

If the language is not phonetic, the teacher can compose separate words with the movable alphabet, and then pronounce them, letting the child repeat by himself the exercise of arranging and rereading them.

In the material there are two movable alphabets. One of them consists of larger letters, and is divided into two boxes, each of which contains the vowels. This is used for the first exercises, in which the child needs very large objects in order to recognize the letters. When he is acquainted with one half of the consonants he can begin to compose words, even though he is dealing with one part only of the alphabet.

The other movable alphabet has smaller letters and is contained in a single box. It is given to children who have made their first attempts at composition with words, and already know the complete alphabet.

It is after these exercises with the movable alphabet that the child *is able to write entire words*. This phenomenon generally occurs unexpectedly, and then a child who has never yet traced a stroke or a letter on paper *writes several words in succession*. From that moment he continues to write, always gradually perfecting himself. This spontaneous writing takes on the characteristics of a *natural* phenomenon, and the child who has begun to write the "first word" will continue to write in the same way as he spoke after pronouncing the first word, and as he walked after having taken the first step. The same course of inner formation through which the phenomenon of writing appeared is the course of his future progress, of his growth to perfection. The child prepared in this way has entered upon a course of development through which he will pass as surely as the growth of the body and the development of the natural functions have passed through their course of development when life has once been established.

For the interesting and very complex phenomena relating to the development of writing and then of reading, see my larger works.

The Reading of Music

FIG. 32.--THE MUSICAL STAFF.[1]

When the child knows how to read, he can make a first application of this knowledge to the reading of the names of musical notes.

In connection with the material for sensory education, consisting of the series of bells, we use a didactic material, which serves as an introduction to musical reading. For this purpose we have, in the first place, a wooden board, not very long, and painted pale green. On this board the staff is cut out in black, and in every line and space are cut round holes, inside each of which is written the name of the note in its reference to the treble clef.

There is also a series of little white discs which can be fitted into the holes. On one side of each disc is written the name of the note (doh, re, mi, fah, soh, lah, ti, doh).

The child, guided by the name written on the discs, puts them, with the name uppermost, in their right places on the board and then reads the names of the notes. This exercise he can do by himself, and he learns the position of each note on the staff. Another exercise which the child can do at the same time is to place the disc bearing the name of the note on the rectangular base of the corresponding bell, whose sound he has already learned to recognize by ear in the sensorial exercise described above.

---

[1] The single staff is used in the Conservatoire of Milan and utilized in the Perlasca method.

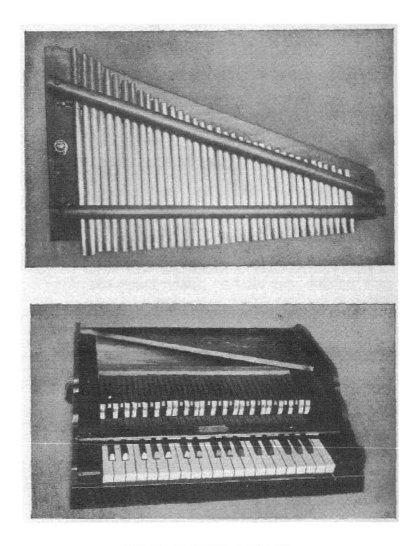

FIG. 39.--DUMB KEYBOARD.

Following this exercise there is another staff made on a board of green wood, which is longer than the other and has neither indentures nor signs. A considerable number of discs, on one side of which are written the names of the notes, is at the disposal of the child. He takes up a disc at random, reads its name and places it on the staff, with the name underneath, so that the white face of the disc shows on the top. By the repetition of this exercise the child is enabled to arrange many discs on the same line or in the same space. When he has finished, he turns them all over so that the names are outside, and so finds out if he has made mistakes. After learning the treble clef the child passes on to learn the bass with great ease.

To the staff described above can be added another similar to it, arranged as is shown in the figure. (Fig. 32.) The child beginning with doh, lays the discs on the board in ascending order in their right position until the octave is reached: doh, re, mi, fah, soh, lah, ti, doh. Then he descends the scale in the same way, returning to *doh*, but continuing to place the discs always to the right: soh, fah, mi, re, doh. In this way he forms an angle. At this point he descends again to the lower staff, ti, lah, soh, fah, mi, re, doh, then he ascends again on the other side: re, mi, fah, soh, lah, ti, and by forming with his two lines of discs another angle in the bass, he has completed a rhombus, "the rhombus of the notes."

After the discs have been arranged in this way, the upper staff is separated from the lower. In the lower the notes are arranged according to the bass clef. In this way the first elements of musical reading are presented to the child, reading which corresponds to *sounds* with which the child's ear is already acquainted.

For a first practical application of this knowledge we have used in our schools a miniature pianoforte keyboard, which reproduces the essentials of this instrument, although in a simplified form, and so that they are visible. Two octaves only are reproduced, and the keys, which are small, are proportioned to the hand of a little child of four or five years, as the keys of the common piano are proportioned to those of the adult. All the mechanism of the key is visible. (Fig. 39.) On striking a key one sees the hammer rise, on which is written the name of the note. The hammers are black and white, like the notes.

With this instrument it is very easy for the child to practice alone, finding the notes on the keyboard corresponding to some bar of written music, and following the movements of the fingers made in playing the piano.

The keyboard in itself is mute, but a series of resonant tubes, resembling a set of organ-pipes, can be applied to the upper surface, so that the hammers striking these produce musical notes corresponding to the keys struck. The child can then pursue his exercises with the control of the musical sounds.

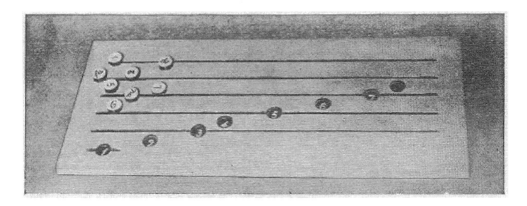

FIG. 33

On the wooden board, round spaces are cut out corresponding to the notes. Inside each of the spaces there is a figure. On one side of each of the discs is written a number and on the other the name of the note. They are fitted by the child into the corresponding places.

FIG. 34.

The child next arranged the discs in the notes cut out on the staff, but there are no longer numbers written to help him find the places. Instead, he must try to remember the place of the note on the staff. If he is not sure he consults the numbered board (Fig. 33).

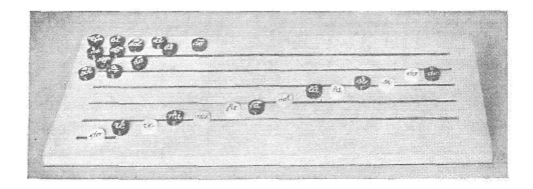

FIG. 35.

The child arranged on the staff the semitones in the spaces which remain where the discs are far apart: do-re, re-mi, fah-soh, soh-la, la-ti. The discs for the semitones have the sharp on one side and the flat on the other, e.g., re[sharp]-mi[flat] are written on the opposite sides of the same disc.

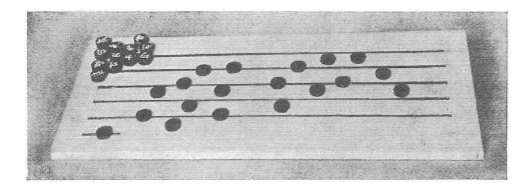

FIG. 36

The children take a large number of discs and arrange them on the staff, leaving uppermost the side which is blank, i.e., the side on which the name of the note is not written. Then they verify their work by turning the discs over and reading the name.

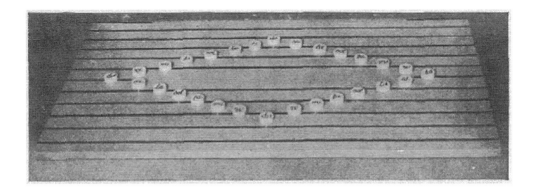

FIG. 37.

The double staff is formed by putting the two staves together. The children arrange the notes in the form of a rhombus.

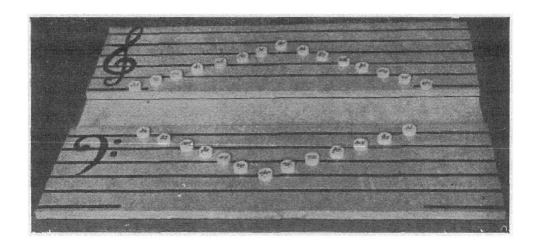

FIG. 38.

The two boards are then separated and the notes remain arranged according to the treble and bass clefs. The corresponding key signatures are then placed upon the two different staves.

Arithmetic

The children possess all the instinctive knowledge necessary as a preparation for clear ideas on numeration. The idea of quantity was inherent in all the material for the education of the senses: longer, shorter, darker, lighter. The conception of identity and of difference formed part of the actual technique of the education of the senses, which began with the recognition of identical objects, and continued with the arrangement in gradation of similar objects. I will make a special illustration of the first exercise with the solid insets, which can be done even by a child of two and a half. When he makes a mistake by putting a cylinder in a hole too large for it, and so leaves *one* cylinder without a place, he instinctively absorbs the idea of the absence of *one* from a continuous series. The child's mind is not prepared for number "by certain preliminary ideas," given in haste by the teacher, but has been prepared for it by a process of formation, by a slow building up of itself.

To enter directly upon the teaching of arithmetic, we must turn to the same didactic material used for the education of the senses.

Let us look at the three sets of material which are presented after the exercises with the solid insets, *i.e.,* the material for teaching *size* (the pink cubes), *thickness* (the brown prisms), and *length* (the green rods). There is a definite relation between the ten pieces of each series. In the material for length the shortest piece is a *unit of measurement* for all the rest; the second piece is double the first, the third is three times the first, etc., and, whilst the scale of length increases by ten centimeters for each piece, the other dimensions remain constant (*i.e.,* the rods all have the same section).

The pieces then stand in the same relation to one another as the natural series of the numbers 1, 2, 3, 4, 5, 6, 7, 8, 9, 10.

In the second series, namely, that which shows *thickness,* whilst the length remains constant, the square section of the prisms varies. The result is that the sides of the square sections vary according to the series of natural numbers, *i.e.,* in the first prism, the square of the section has sides of one centimeter, in the second of two centimeters, in the third of three centimeters, etc., and so on until the tenth, in which the square of the section has sides of ten centimeters. The prisms therefore are in the same proportion to one another as the numbers of the series of squares (1, 4, 9, etc.), for it would take four prisms of the first size to make the second, nine to make the third, etc. The pieces which make up the series for teaching thickness are therefore in the following proportion: 1 : 4 : 9 : 16 : 25 : 36 : 49 : 64 : 81 : 100.

In the case of the pink cubes the edge increases according to the numerical series, *i.e.,* the first cube has an edge of one centimeter, the second of two centimeters, the third of three centimeters, and so on, to the tenth cube, which has an edge of ten centimeters. Hence the relation in volume between them is that of the cubes of the series of numbers from one to ten, *i.e.*, 1 : 8: 27 : 64: 125 : 216 : 343 : 512 : 729 : 1000. In fact, to make up the volume of the second pink cube, eight of the first little cubes would be required; to make up the volume of the third, twenty-seven would be required, and so on.

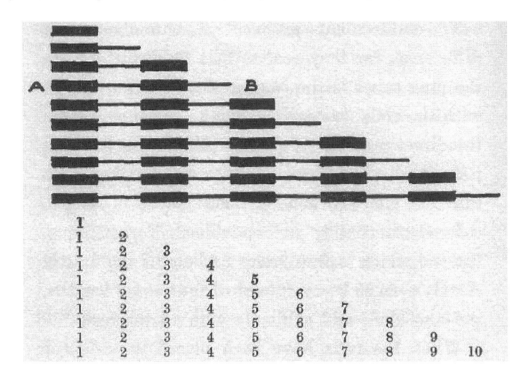

FIG. 40.--DIAGRAM ILLUSTRATING USE OF NUMERICAL RODS.

The children have an intuitive knowledge of this difference, for they realize that the exercise with the pink cubes is the *easiest* of all three and that with the rods the most difficult. When we begin the direct teaching of number, we choose the long rods, modifying them, however, by dividing them into ten spaces, each ten centimeters in length, colored alternately red and blue. For example, the rod which is four times as long as the first is clearly seen to be composed of four equal lengths, red and blue; and similarly with all the rest.

When the rods have been placed in order of gradation, we teach the child the numbers: one, two, three, etc., by touching the rods in succession, from the first up to ten. Then, to help him to gain a clear idea of number, we proceed to the recognition of separate rods by means of the customary lesson in three periods.

We lay the three first rods in front of the child, and pointing to them or taking them in the hand in turn, in order to show them to him we say: "This is *one*." "This is *two*." "This is *three*." We point out with the finger the divisions in each rod, counting them so as to make sure, "One, two: this is *two*." "One, two, three: this is *three*." Then we say to the child: "Give me *two*." "Give me *one*." "Give me *three*." Finally, pointing to a rod, we say, "What is this?" The child answers, "Three," and we count together: "One, two, three."

In the same way we teach all the other rods in their order, adding always one or two more according to the responsiveness of the child.

The importance of this didactic material is that it gives a clear idea of *number*. For when a number is named it exists as an object, a unity in itself. When we say that a man possesses a million, we mean that he has a *fortune* which is worth so many units of measure of values, and these units all belong to one person.

So, if we add 7 to 8 (7 + 8), we add a *number to a number*, and these numbers for a *definite* reason represent in themselves groups of homogeneous units.

Again, when the child shows us the 9, he is handling a rod which is inflexible--an object complete in itself, yet composed of *nine equal parts* which can be counted. And when he comes to add 8 to 2, he will place next to one another, two rods, two objects, one of which has eight equal lengths and the other two. When, on the other hand, in ordinary schools, to make the calculation easier, they present the child with different objects to count, such as beans, marbles, etc., and when, to take the case I have quoted (8 + 2), he takes a group of eight marbles and adds two more marbles to it, the natural impression in his mind is not that he has added 8 to 2, but that he has added 1 + 1 + 1 + 1 + 1 + 1 + 1 + 1 to 1 + 1. The result is not so clear, and the child is required to make the effort of holding in his mind the idea of a group of eight objects as *one united whole*, corresponding to a single number, 8.

This effort often puts the child back, and delays his understanding of number by months or even years.

The addition and subtraction of numbers under ten are made very much simpler by the use of the didactic material for teaching lengths. Let the child be presented with the attractive problem of arranging the pieces in such a way as to have a set of rods, all as long as the longest. He first arranges the rods in their right order (the long stair); he then takes the last rod (1) and lays it next to the 9. Similarly, he takes the last rod but one (2) and lays it next to the 8, and so on up to the 5.

This very simple game represents the addition of numbers within the ten: 9 + 1, 8 + 2, 7 + 3, 6 + 4. Then, when he puts the rods back in their places, he must first take away the 4 and put it back under the 5, and then take away in their turn the 3, the 2, the 1. By this action he has put the rods back again in their right gradation, but he has also performed a series of arithmetical subtractions, 10 - 4, 10 - 3, 10 - 2, 10 - 1.

The teaching of the actual figures marks an advance from the rods to the process of counting with separate units. When the figures are known, they will serve the very purpose in the abstract which the rods serve in the concrete; that is, they will stand for the *uniting into one whole* of a certain number of separate units.

[83]

The *synthetic* function of language and the wide field of work which it opens out for the intelligence is *demonstrated*, we might say, by the function of the *figure*, which now can be substituted for the concrete rods.

The use of the actual rods only would limit arithmetic to the small operations within the ten or numbers a little higher, and, in the construction of the mind, these operations would advance very little farther than the limits of the first simple and elementary education of the senses.

The figure, which is a word, a graphic sign, will permit of that unlimited progress which the mathematical mind of man has been able to make in the course of its evolution.

In the material there is a box containing smooth cards, on which are gummed the figures from one to nine, cut out in sandpaper. These are analogous to the cards on which are gummed the sandpaper letters of the alphabet. The method of teaching is always the same. The child is *made to touch* the figures in the direction in which they are written, and to name them at the same time.

In this case he does more than when he learned the letters; he is shown how to place each figure upon the corresponding rod. When all the figures have been learned in this way, one of the first exercises will be to place the number cards upon the rods arranged in gradation. So arranged, they form a succession of steps on which it is a pleasure to place the cards, and the children remain for a long time repeating this intelligent game.

After this exercise comes what we may call the "emancipation" of the child. He carried his own figures with him, and now *using them* he will know how to group units together.

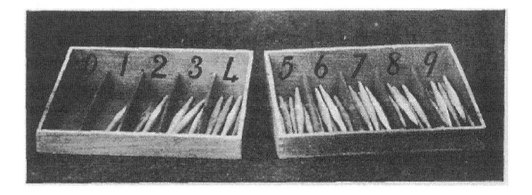

FIG. 41.--COUNTING BOXES.

For this purpose we have in the didactic material a series of wooden pegs, but in addition to these we give the children all sorts of small objects--sticks, tiny cubes, counters, etc.

The exercise will consist in placing opposite a figure the number of objects that it indicates. The child for this purpose can use the box which is included in the material. (Fig. 41.) This box is divided into compartments, above each of which is printed a figure and the child places in the compartment the corresponding number of pegs.

Another exercise is to lay all the figures on the table and place below them the corresponding number of cubes, counters, etc.

This is only the first step, and it would be impossible here to speak of the succeeding lessons in zero, in tens and in other arithmetical processes--for the development of which my larger works must be consulted. The didactic material itself, however, can give some idea. In the box containing the pegs there is one compartment over which the 0 is printed. Inside this compartment "nothing must be put," and then we begin with *one.*

Zero is nothing, but it is placed next to one to enable us to count when we pass beyond 9--thus, 10.

FIG. 42.--ARITHMETIC FRAME.

If, instead of the piece 1, we were to take pieces as long as the rod 10, we could count 10, 20, 30, 40, 50, 60, 70, 80, 90. In the didactic material there are frames containing cards on which are printed such numbers from 10 to 90. These numbers are fixed into a frame in such a way that the figures 1 to 9 can be slipped in covering the zero. If the zero of 10 is covered by 1 the result is 11, if with 2 it becomes 12, and so on, until the last 9. Then we pass to the twenties (the second ten), and so on, from ten to ten. (Fig. 42.)

For the beginning of this exercise with the cards marking the tens we can use the rods. As we begin with the first ten (10) in the frame, we take the rod 10. We then place the small rod 1 next to rod 10, and at the same time slip in the number 1, covering the zero of the 10. Then we take rod 1 and figure 1 away from the frame, and put in their place rod 2 next to rod 10, and figure 2 over the zero in the frame, and so on, up to 9. To advance farther we should need to use two rods of 10 to make 20.

The children show much enthusiasm when learning these exercises, which demand from them two sets of activities, and give them in their work clearness of idea.

* * * * *

In writing and arithmetic we have gathered the fruits of a laborious education which consisted in coordinating the movements and gaining a first knowledge of the world. This culture comes as a natural consequence of man's first efforts to put himself into intelligent communication with the world.

All those early acquisitions which have brought order into the child's mind, would be wasted were they not firmly established by means of written language and of figures. Thus established, however, these experiences open up an unlimited field for future education. What we have done, therefore, is to introduce the child to a higher level--the level of culture--and he will now be able to pass on to a *school*, but not the school we know to-day, where, irrationally, we try to give culture to minds not yet prepared or *educated to receive it.*

To preserve the health of their minds, which have been *exercised* and not *fatigued* by the order of the work, our children must have a new kind of school for the acquisition of culture. My experiments in the continuation of this method for older children are already far advanced.

Moral Factors

A brief description such as this, of the *means* which are used in the "Children's House," may perhaps give the reader the impression of a logical and convincing system of education. But the importance of my method does not lie in the organization itself, but *in the effects which it produces on the child*. It is the *child* who proves the value of this method by his spontaneous manifestations, which seem to reveal the laws of man's inner development.[2] Psychology will perhaps find in the "Children's Houses" a laboratory which will bring more truths to light than thus hitherto recognized; for the essential factor in psychological research, especially in the field of psychogenesis, the origin and development of the mind, must be the establishment of normal conditions for the free development of thought.

---

[2] See the chapters on Discipline in my larger works.

Postface

As is well known, we leave the children *free* in their work, and in all actions which are not of a disturbing kind. That is, we *eliminate* disorder, which is "bad," but allow to that which is orderly and "good" the most complete liberty of manifestation.

The results obtained are surprising, for the children have shown a love of work which no one suspected to be in them, and a calm and an orderliness in their movements which, surpassing the limits of correctness have entered into those of "grace." The spontaneous discipline, and the obedience which is seen in the whole class, constitute the most striking result of our method.

The ancient philosophical discussion as to whether man is born good or evil is often brought forward in connection with my method, and many who have supported it have done so on the ground that it provides a demonstration of man's natural goodness. Very many others, on the contrary, have opposed it, considering that to leave children free is a dangerous mistake, since they have in them innate tendencies to evil.

I should like to put the question upon a more positive plane.

In the words "good" and "evil" we include the most varying ideas, and we confuse them especially *in our practical dealings with little children.*

The tendencies which we stigmatize as *evil* in little children of three to six years of age are often merely those which cause *annoyance* to us adults when, not understanding their needs, we try to prevent their *every movement*, their every *attempt to gain experience for themselves in the world* (by touching everything, etc.). The child, however, through this *natural tendency*, is led to *coordinate his movements* and to collect impressions, especially sensations of touch, so that when prevented he *rebels*, and this rebellion forms almost the whole of his "naughtiness."

What wonder is it that the evil disappears when, if we give the right *means* for development and leave full liberty to use them, rebellion has no more reason for existence?

Further, by the substitution of a series of outbursts of *joy* for the old series of outbursts of *rage*, the moral physiognomy of the child comes to assume a calm and gentleness which make him appear a different being.

It is we who provoked the children to the violent manifestations of a real *struggle for existence*. In order to exist *according to the needs of their psychic development* they were often obliged to snatch from us the things which seemed necessary to them for the purpose. They had to move contrary to our laws, or sometimes to struggle with other children to wrest from them the objects of their desire.

On the other hand, if we give children the *means of existence*, the struggle for it disappears, and a vigorous expansion of life takes its place. This question involves a hygienic principle connected with the nervous system during the difficult period when the brain is still rapidly growing, and should be of great interest to specialists in children's diseases and nervous derangements. The inner life of man and the beginnings of his intellect are controlled by special laws and vital necessities which cannot be forgotten if we are aiming at health for mankind.

For this reason, an educational method, which cultivates and protects the inner activities of the child, is not a question which concerns merely the school or the teachers; it is a universal question which concerns the family, and is of vital interest to mothers.

To go more deeply into a question is often the only means of answering it rightly. If, for instance, we were to see men fighting over a piece of bread, we might say: "How bad men are!" If, on the other hand, we entered a well-warmed eating-house, and saw them quietly finding a place and choosing their meal without any envy of one another, we might say: "How good men are!" Evidently, the question of absolute good and evil, intuitive ideas of which guide us in our superficial judgment, goes beyond such limitations as these. We can, for instance, provide excellent eating-houses for an entire people without directly affecting the question of their morals. One might say, indeed, that to judge by appearances, a well-fed people are *better, quieter, and commit less crime* than a nation that is ill-nourished; but whoever draws from that the conclusion that to make men good it is *enough* to feed them, will be making an obvious mistake.

It cannot be denied, however, that *nourishment* will be an essential factor in obtaining goodness, in the sense that it will *eliminate* all the *evil acts, and the bitterness* caused by lack of bread.

Now, in our case, we are dealing with a far deeper need--the nourishment of man's inner life, and of his higher functions. The bread that we are dealing with is the bread of the spirit, and we are entering into the difficult subject of the satisfaction of man's psychic needs.

We have already obtained a most interesting result, in that we have found it possible to present *new means* of enabling children to reach a higher level of calm and goodness, and we have been able to establish these means by experience. The whole foundation of our results rests upon these means which we have discovered, and which may be divided under two heads--the *organization of work*, and liberty.

It is the perfect organization of work, permitting the possibility of self-development and giving outlet for the energies, which procures for each child the beneficial and calming *satisfaction*. And it is under such conditions of work that liberty leads to a perfecting of the activities, and to the attainment of a fine discipline which is in itself the result of that new quality of *calmness* that has been developed in the child.

Freedom without organization of work would be useless. The child left *free* without means of work would go to waste, just as a new-born baby, if *left free* without nourishment, would die of starvation. *The organization of the work*, therefore, is the corner-stone of this new structure of goodness; but even that organization would be in vain without the *liberty* to make use of it, and without freedom for the expansion of all those energies which spring from the satisfaction of the child's highest activities.

Has not a similar phenomenon occurred also in the history of man? The history of civilization is a history of successful attempts to organize work and to obtain liberty. On the whole, man's goodness has also increased, as is shown by his progress from barbarism to civilization, and it may be said that crime, the various forms of wickedness, cruelty and violence have been gradually decreasing during this passage of time.

The *criminality* of our times, as a matter of fact, has been compared to a form of *barbarism* surviving in the midst of civilized peoples. It is, therefore, through the better organization of work that society will probably attain to a further purification, and in the meanwhile it seems unconsciously to be seeking the overthrow of the last barriers between itself and liberty.

If this is what we learn from society, how great should be the results among little children from three to six years of age if the organization of their work is complete, and their freedom absolute? It is for this reason that to us they seem so good, like heralds of hope and of redemption.

If men, walking as yet so painfully and imperfectly along the road of work and of freedom, have become better, why should we fear that the same road will prove disastrous to the children?

Yet, on the other hand, I would not say that the goodness of our little ones in their freedom will solve the problem of the absolute goodness or wickedness of man. We can only say that we have made a contribution to the cause of goodness by removing obstacles which were the cause of violence and of rebellion.

Let us "render, therefore, unto Cæsar the things that are Cæsar's, and unto God the things that are God's."

4986007R0

Made in the USA
Lexington, KY
22 March 2010